About the Author:

FRED SMITH, SR. is an internationally noted author, speaker, and
management consultant who has
advised and mentored leaders for
nearly sixty years. An executive with
GENESCO for many years, Smith is a
contributing editor to LEADERSHIP
and recently retired from the board
of directors of Christianity Today, Inc.

About the General Editor:

DAVID L. GOETZ is editor of
LEADERSHIP Resources, a division of
LEADERSHIP, the most respected
journal in America for pastors and
church leaders.

Leading With Integrity

THE PASTOR'S SOUL SERIES
DAVID L. GOETZ • GENERAL EDITOR

The Power of Loving Your Church
David Hansen

Pastoral Grit
Craig Brian Larson

Preaching With Spiritual Passion
Ed Rowell

Listening to the Voice of God
Roger Barrier

Leading With Integrity
Fred Smith, Sr.

LIBRARY OF LEADERSHIP DEVELOPMENT
MARSHALL SHELLEY • GENERAL EDITOR

Leading Your Church Through Conflict and Reconciliation
Renewing Your Church Through Vision and Planning
Building Your Church Through Counsel and Care
Growing Your Church Through Training and Motivation

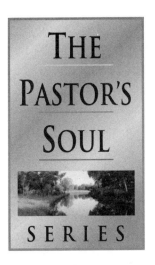

THE
PASTOR'S
SOUL

SERIES

Leading With Integrity

FRED·SMITH, SR.

David L. Goetz · General Editor

BETHANY HOUSE PUBLISHERS
MINNEAPOLIS, MINNESOTA 55438

Leading With Integrity
Copyright © 1999
Fred Smith, Sr.

Cover by Dan Thornberg,
Bethany House Publishers staff artist.

Published by Bethany House Publishers
A Ministry of Bethany Fellowship International
11400 Hampshire Avenue South
Minneapolis, Minnesota 55438
www.bethanyhouse.com

Printed in the United States of America by
Bethany Press International, Minneapolis, Minnesota 55438

ISBN 1–55661–971–5

FRED SMITH, SR., is a noted author, speaker, and management consultant who has been advising and mentoring leaders for sixty years. A recipient of the Lawrence Appley Award of the American Management Association, he has lectured internationally on the philosophy of leadership and has been awarded two honorary doctorates. He has served as chair of four national ministry boards, including Youth for Christ and Key Life.

Fred is currently director emeritus of Christianity Today, Inc., after twenty-two years of board service. Broadly published, Fred Smith is a contributing editor to LEADERSHIP. He is the author of *You and Your Network* and *Learning to Lead*. He has been a guest on *Focus on the Family, Hour of Power, The 700 Club,* and *Successful Texans.* He is the father of three grown children, six grandchildren, and one great-grandchild. He lives in Dallas with Mary Alice, his wife of more than six decades.

ACKNOWLEDGMENTS

May I thank all those who through the long years have shaped my thinking and focused my activities as well as those who have repeatedly worked on the manuscript, especially Margie Keith, my secretary, who for nineteen years was Maxey Jarman's private secretary, and Kevin A. Miller and David Goetz, for patiently squeezing the material out of a recalcitrant author.

My appreciation to Dr. John Maxwell, insightful apostle of leadership, who first got me to formulate my principles of mentoring, and to my friend William R. Waugh, Dallas entrepreneur who introduced me to François Fenelon.

I am particularly grateful for the cooperation of my family: Mary Alice, my wife of sixty-two years, and our three mature children, Brenda, Fred Jr., and Mary Helen, all of whom challenge and encourage my thinking.

Bless you all.

PREFACE

My friend Fred—actually, he's more than a friend. He's a confidant, adviser, mentor, pleasant companion, and encourager. He has guided me through some deep water; given me wise counsel; answered some of my puzzling life, scriptural, and business questions; and provided me with a wealth of material for my books and seminars—so much so that it's been years since I've written a book that did not include a few "Smithisms."

Leading With Integrity is an extension of Fred Smith's love for mentoring others but especially for those who aspire to spread the gospel of Christ. You will note his economy of words as he serves up helping after helping of common sense, wise and thought-provoking pearls that inspire and convict you to *be* more so you can do more.

Fred writes to you as he has talked to me since he took me under his wings years ago. At our first meeting, I had to use scraps of paper to record his gems of wisdom. Since then I've always brought a notepad to record his "message" for the occasion. He always gives me usable, transferable ideas.

One dinner session, however, says it all about Fred Smith—about who he is, and what he does, and where his heart is. That night Fred loaded me with wisdom, ideas, and insights, which filled much of my notepad.

I said, "Fred, you should put this in a book."

He smiled and said, "I've got a better idea. I want my friend Zig Ziglar to put it in a book."

His agenda is to honor Christ and to serve people by teaching them how to love God more and how to serve him and his children better. *Leading With Integrity* accomplishes that objective. When I read the manuscript, I later noted that I had underlined or bracketed provocative thoughts, procedures, or pearls of wisdom on ninety-seven pages. I was tempted to include a few of them in this preface but didn't because there are so many it is impossible to select the best.

I predict that *Leading With Integrity* will become a permanent part of your life. Smithisms will become a part of your vocabulary, and most of this book will be underlined. It's good—really good.

—Zig Ziglar
October 1998

CONTENTS

INTRODUCTION

IN A REAL SENSE, LEADERSHIP in industry is different than leadership in Christ's church. Writer M. Scott Peck once asked me, "Why don't you businessmen take over the church?"

"Because we can't lead a spiritual church successfully," I said. "Secular principles that are not anointed by the Holy Spirit are not applicable to the church. In fact, they can pollute it by bypassing the Spirit."

Some principles can be transferred when they are spiritually ordained, and over the years I have been associated with some fine leaders in industry as well as in Christian work. *Leading With Integrity*, however, grew out of my sense that today in the institutional church we've become almost too dependent on human leadership principles. We know a great deal about effective organization through extensive research.

My concern is that in the church we may be trying to do God's work in man's way.

In *Leading With Integrity*, I investigate the question, "As we go about our work, what are we responsible for, and what do we depend on God for?" One principle I've learned is that God will not do for me what I can do for myself, but he will not let me do for myself what only he can do. God has given me intelligence and created my opportunities—I have a responsibility to use my gifts fully. If I'm not willing to do that, God has no obligation to add his blessing to what I do. On the other hand, when I try to accomplish by human means what can be done only by spiritual means, I embezzle God's authority.

For example, no amount of carefully planned evangelistic campaigns will win souls to Christ. Only the Holy Spirit wins a soul. Nevertheless, that doesn't let us off the hook. We still have to employ the highest and most dedicated talent in seeking the lost. But winning a soul, we cannot do. We can collect numbers and add names to the membership rolls, but we cannot add names to the Lamb's Book of Life. God alone can inscribe those.

If we are to do God's work God's way, we must start with character. In *Leading With Integrity*, I set out principles that leaders can use to examine their character and the character of those whom they lead. Christian leaders need to examine themselves, so that with the apostle Paul they can say, "Follow me as I follow Christ."

Unfortunately we are not as conscious of our character flaws as we are of our inadequacies in the areas of knowledge and experience. In my sixty years in business, nobody has said, "I have a flawed character." It is much easier to admit a lack of skill than to admit to a character weakness. Yet from 75 to 80 percent of the failures I've seen have been character failures.

The church must be involved in character building, helping men and women to grow into the maturity of Christ. Leaders are responsible for modeling and encouraging character and integrity. Dr. Howard Rome, head of psychiatry at Mayo Clinic in Rochester, Minnesota, gave me a book in which he wrote: "Few men have the imagination to grasp the truth of reality." I trust this book will stir not only your imagination but your faith to grasp the truth and reality of our potential—to be awakened to the truth of Christlikeness in us.

To women leaders: While I try to think inclusively, I admit my vocabulary is historically male. I am trying to improve. Part of the maleness of my writing is that I had, early on, all male teachers. I had not met or observed the many excellent women leaders I came to know. Here are a few of them: Mildred Custin, CEO of Bonwit Teller; Gerry Stutz, CEO, Henri Bendel; Evelyn Nelson, Partner, Russell Stover Candy; Helen Van Slyke, CEO, House of Fragrance; and chief among those whom I admire, the gracious, capable Mary Crowley, founder of Home Interiors.

I have found that women learn and adapt to relational leadership more naturally than men. Your intuition is generally much better than ours, your desire for good relationships is stronger, and your vision just as expansive. You lead with so much subtlety and finesse. You seem to do things right because it is the right thing to do. So often I did so awkwardly what you do so gracefully. I will continually learn from you.

I was interviewing a prospective corporate president, and at the close of the interview I asked him, "What's your ultimate aim?" He grew quiet. I sensed he was deciding to tell me the truth.

"My ultimate aim," he said, "is that when I face the

Lord, he will say, 'Well done, thou good and faithful servant.' "

There is no finer ambition. May this book help you as a leader to continue as a good, faithful servant to our Lord.

PART I

BECOMING A WHOLE PERSON

1

NIGHT DIALOGUES

SELF-RESPECT IS THE KEY INDICATOR of our integrity as a person. Without personal integrity, it is impossible to have integrity in leading others.

Defining self-respect is difficult, yet it is the most important of all forms of respect. It is the foundation of our accepting any other respect. We feel tentative about the respect that comes from others until we genuinely respect ourselves.

After I spoke to a group of corporate officers, several of us gathered around for a bull session. One of the CEOs, with his tongue loosened by spirits from a bottle, said, "Fred, you talk a lot about self-respect. How do you define it?"

"I can't give you a dictionary definition," I said, "but I can tell you how I know I've got it. When I wake up at three o'clock in the morning, I talk to the little guy inside me who is still simple, honest, and knows right from wrong. He hasn't rationalized enough to become sophisticated. He still sees things in black and white. He is the 'honest me.'

When we can talk freely, I know we respect who I am. When he turns away and won't talk to me, I know I'm in trouble. If he says, 'Get lost, you're a phony,' I know that I've lost my self-respect."

Instantly the CEO jumped out of his chair, circled it, and said, "Man, you done plowed up a snake!" Evidently his night dialogues were troubling him. A few months later, I understood his response better when I read he was under investigation.

Integrity is based in character. It cost me a lot of money in a bad investment to learn that character is more important in leadership than intelligence. I had mistakenly put intelligence above character. Intelligence is important, but character is more important. One of America's wealthiest investors said at Harvard that the three qualities he looks for in those with whom he will invest his money are character, intelligence, and energy.

Character is so important because it cannot be fully evaluated but will fail at the time when we can least afford it. It is almost impossible to buttress weak character.

My experience has brought me to a controversial belief about character: Character is sectionalized like a grapefruit, not homogeneous like a bottle of milk. When we say a person has a strong character or a weak character, we assume that their character is of one piece of cloth. I have not found this to be true. Some totally honest in business are hypocritical in personal life. Some are trustworthy in one section of their life and untrustworthy in another. It has been important to my leadership that I build on the solid parts of a person's character. Few people indeed have all good sections, and few have no good sections at all. I've always been intrigued by the story that Willie Sutton, the bank robber, cried when he had to lie to his mother about where he was. Criminals often exhibit impeccable loyalty to their own. Gang members will die for their gang. They will endure torture to maintain confidentiality.

Fortunately, God is the great strengthener of character. As the ancients say, God polishes his saints with tribulation, suffering, trials, and silence. I am convinced that God is much more interested in our character than he is in our intelligence, for character is of the heart. Scripture says, "Out of the heart come the issues of life."

In my night dialogues with the little guy inside me, I have found that certain questions have become channel markers in my search for integrity.

Does my motive have integrity?

Integrity starts with motive. I can't be totally honest, for I am sinful, but I can avoid being dishonest. Dishonesty is a decision.

Rationalization does more to pollute our integrity of motive than any other thing. Rationalization attempts to excuse our lack of integrity. We repeatedly hear "Everyone is doing it," or "Times have changed. This is the new way." Again, "I had no choice if I wanted to win," or "I had to go along with the majority to stay in fellowship."

The justification for rationalization is that wrong ultimately will serve a good purpose. But in God's economy, the end never justifies the means. God is more interested in the process than the product, since he is sovereign. It is the process that produces our maturity in Christ, which is his chief concern.

After we rationalize our behavior to ourselves and to others, soon we try to rationalize it with God. That changes confession into explanation.

Am I ego-driven or responsibility-motivated?

When I asked a director of the entrepreneurial school at SMU, "What are the common denominators of entrepreneurs?" she said, "Number one, they want to be in control. Number two, they want to be accomplishing."

After thinking about that, I wanted to ask her whether this drive to control and accomplish is ego-based or driven by a sense of responsibility. I have known leaders with both motives. The greatest differences between the two types of leaders are the spirit from which they operate and their attitude toward others. Ego-driven people satisfy their ego from the cause, while responsibility-motivated people sacrifice their ego to the cause. Ego-drivenness lacks Christian integrity.

A friend was chairman of future planning for a large church. When he asked the pastor if there were any limitations to the planning, the pastor said, "The church cannot be moved during my lifetime." The pastor's ego superseded the ultimate good of the organization. The planning had to satisfy his ego. The leader of an organization often must ask, "Is this decision based on my ego or my sense of responsibility?"

The inimitable Gert Behanna said it this way: "Is it for

God or for Gert? If it's for God, I do it. If it's for Gert, I don't."

Do I want the truth?

It requires a tough mind and a strong heart to love truth, no matter where it comes from. When we are selective in accepting truth, we are not genuine lovers of truth.

A friend had lunch with a non-practicing Jew who brought up the subject of religion. His Jewish friend said he wanted his son to study comparative religion so that when he became a man he could make an informed choice. My friend asked, "Would you yourself accept truth if you found it?" He quickly said, "No. Truth is too scary."

Christian communicator Steve Brown recently visited with a well-known TV talk-show host at a social luncheon. The latter was not a believer. He asked Steve to explain Christianity. Before doing so, Steve asked, "If I explain it to you so that you have to say that it makes sense, will you become a Christian?"

The TV host said, "No."

"Then I won't waste my time," Steve replied, "explaining something that you've already rejected with a closed mind."

I once talked with a scientist from Oxford University who had become a Christian. He wanted his roommate to accept Christ. While this scientist had thoughtfully explained to his roommate over a two-year period the claims of Christ, always to be rejected, his roommate finally said, "If I wanted to believe, I would. I don't want to believe."

Truth can be warped by tradition, interpretation, cliché, or current thought. Truth demands I try to know and love it for its own sake. That requires I have an ever-expanding understanding of truth and an open mind to discern truth with intellectual integrity, yet hold to the sure proposition that all human truth is flawed. The only perfect truth is the revealed truth: "I am the truth," Jesus said. Without this fixed point, we easily wander off into the fallacy of relative truth, confusing human *veritas* with divine revelation.

Am I the pump or the pipe?

I led a lay retreat for a few hundred men in the mountains near Fresno, California. The retreat began on a Friday night and ended Sunday noon; I was the only speaker. That fact came as a surprise when I arrived to speak. Late Sunday afternoon while on a plane returning to Dallas, I wondered how I could feel so normal after such a strenuous weekend. Generally I am either higher than a kite or lower than a snake's belt buckle. Instead, I felt like I had just finished a day's work at the office.

From that experience I learned that with God's presence permeating the meetings, he was the source; I was only the spokesman. In other words, God was the pump, and I was the pipe. The pipe never gets tired. When I attempt to be the pump as well as the pipe, that takes more than I have. When I try to substitute my power for God's, I become powerless, dissatisfied, even frantic and defeated.

A few years back, Mary Alice and I were listening to a series of sermons by a well-known young minister who has since left the ministry. When she asked what I thought of him, I told her that I greatly admired his technical ability, his research, his eloquence and delivery, but I never sensed in his sermons spiritual power. I felt he was spiritually impotent. I kept wanting to feel the presence of the Spirit, which I never did. He later divorced his wife and left the ministry, not from lack of talent, with which he was greatly blessed, but from lack of spiritual power. The apostle Paul said, "I came not in excellence of words but in power."

The secret is expressed in Jim May's book, *In His Place*, in which he asks the question, "Are you working for God or is he working through you?" Too few are the times when I fully realize that God is using me, that what I am doing is his working through me rather than my working for him.

Those who become Christian celebrities must be careful that they don't cross over the line from realizing that God is using them to thinking they are being recognized by God for their great potential contribution. We are not to be volunteers, selecting our service for God, but dedicates, letting God select our service. When God selects, he sends power. When we volunteer, we keep control, even while attempting worthwhile work.

Seventeenth-century spirituality writer Michael Molinos warned,

> The sermons and messages of men who have a great deal of learning and information but who lack an experiential knowledge of the internal things of the Spirit—such men can make up many stories, give elegant descriptions, acute discourses, elaborate theses, and yet regardless of how much it seems to be grounded in the Scripture, what these men give us does not contain the word of God. It is but the words of men adulterated with false gold. Such men actually corrupt

Christians, feeding them with wind and with vanity. As a result both the teacher and the one taught remain empty of their God.[1]

Does my will control my feelings?

Integrity is more a matter of the will than of feelings. Certainly feelings are important, for without feelings we become mechanical. We are not able to connect with others or to feel empathy or compassion. Feelings energize us. They are great implementers but poor leaders. Our will must control our feelings.

Our will is the single most distinguishing feature of our character. I was fortunate to have a mother with an indomitable will. In spite of many physical disabilities, she persevered, often quoting Galatians 6:9: "Be not weary in well doing, for in due season you shall reap if you faint not." It was from her that we chose as a family motto that little phrase inspired by Rudyard Kipling's "If": "When nothing but your will says go."

I remember when my mother was so sick she had to put ladderback chairs around the kitchen so she could fall from one chair to the other while she prepared meals for her family. She was indomitable, the unsinkable Molly Brown. I profited a great deal from her example; I went through twelve years of public school without missing a day. I was never encouraged to "take it easy."

Leadership demands a strong will—not a selfish or stubborn will, but a determined will to do what needs

---

[1]Michael Molinos, *The Spiritual Guide* (Sargent, Ga.: The Seedsowers, 1982).

doing. By will we overcome our yen for pleasure and our satisfaction with mediocrity. Our Catholic friends believe in "substitutionary grace," in which the priest earns grace for the flock. I won't argue this theological point, but I will contend there is substitutionary will, which the leader must give to those in the organization who lack will. A strong will does not blind us to the importance of emotion. It does, however, wring out the rationalization and procrastination that attack us.

Our will, not our feelings, must be charged with the ultimate responsibility for our actions.

Is grace real for me?

Grace was genuine, real, personal, and palpable to the great saints. Brother Lawrence, Frank Laubach, François Fenelon—these Christian mystics had no doubt they were the constant recipients of God's amazing grace. Grace was a practical part of their everyday life. For example, Brother Lawrence said that when he made a mistake he didn't spend any time thinking about it; he just confessed it and moved on. He reminded God that without him, to fall is natural. Before I read that, I lingered over guilt. Immediate grace was too good to be true. Brother Lawrence's experience greatly released me.

Nevertheless, legalism appeals to our common sense. I find it necessary to remind myself that the very Scripture that makes me know my guilt lets me know God's grace. By refusing grace, we play God and punish ourselves. We view events as punishment. We see discipline coming when in reality it isn't discipline, it's just a consequence, but we try to read into it God's judgment.

Why? Because we feel we deserve judgment rather than grace. Grace brings freedom. If only we could accept grace fully, then we, like Brother Lawrence, could have the freedom to admit failure and move on. Since grace cannot be deserved, why should I feel others are more worthy of it than I?

What is my source of joy?

An individual must have hope and joy to live abundantly. Bob Seiple, former head of World Vision, said, "Hope is what we are giving the world. Our help is more than help, it is hope." We can endure almost anything as long as we have hope. When hope is gone, life is gone.

Hope expresses itself in joy. My personal definition of joy is "adequacy." This is the feeling expressed in the old saying, "Nothin' ain't gonna come my way that you and me can't handle, is there, Lord?" That is the joy of true security. With some, joy is effervescent, with others, quiet. But either way, it is the assurance of adequacy.

Without joy, life can become difficult. Sometimes we try to avoid the ache in our heart from the lack of joy by creating synthetic joy, which is never adequate. Without genuine joy it is so easy to fall into despondency when our faith seems not to work for us, while we tell people that it will work for them. This can play havoc in our lives. I have the deepest compassion for those pastors who fall into immorality. They are not hypocrites, they are desperate leaders who have lost the joy of spiritual ministry, substituting for it the synthetic joy of illicit sexuality.

The same synthetic joy can come in the drive for success. Church growth based on ego and ambition may be exciting, but it cannot be joyful in the biblical sense. No matter how far our ambition and ego take us, we ultimately will face that consequence: "He gave them their desire but with it sent leanness of soul."

Joy is a result of seeing God's power work. Often this joy comes in its deepest form during times of great temptation or sorrow. Malcolm Muggeridge, the British intellectual who was a latecomer to Christianity, said in the latter part of his life that as he looked back over his life, he could see no growth in any area except during difficult times. Joy is more than pleasure; it is complete adequacy.

Is my love of God growing?

From childhood I have had a lot of awe of God, but I've never been happy with my love of God. Once at Laity Lodge in the hill country of Texas, three of us friends were holding forth on our knowledge of comparative religions. The wife of one of the men, not known for her scholarship, was half-heartedly listening when she interrupted, "I don't understand a thing you all are talking about. All I know is I love Jesus." At that moment, I would have swapped everything I knew for what I recognized as her deep love for the Lord.

Some friends and I are currently studying how we can deepen our love for the Lord. We know that obedience is evidence of that, but what produces the growth? I believe that if I genuinely appreciate what Christ has done for me, my love for him will increasingly grow.

Someone has said that gratitude is the weakest of all

emotions. We do not stay grateful because that makes us indebted, and we don't want to be indebted. The biblical phrase "sacrifice of thanksgiving" was a puzzle to me until I realized that gratitude is acknowledging that someone did something for me that I could not do for myself. Gratitude expresses our vulnerability, our dependence on others. Sometimes a person whom you have helped through a severe problem will, following the solution, draw away. In some pernicious way, seeing those who supported us can remind us of the problem.

On the other hand, I have found people with deep gratitude often develop deep love. One of my fondest memories involves a young man who had never made more than $15,000 a year yet was extremely talented. Three others and I backed him financially. Within a year he was making $100,000 a year, and since then he has made millions. His gratitude has deepened into genuine love.

He was deserted by his father when he was very young, causing him to suffer abject poverty. Today he refers to me as his father. I am proud to have him as a foster son and a great friend.

When my wife, Mary Alice, had a brain tumor removed at the Mayo Clinic, I got a call from him the night before surgery. When I asked where he was, he said he was down in the lobby. "What are you doing down there?" I asked. He said, "I want to sit with you and the family during the operation." He had flown in to spend that four-and-a-half hours with us.

I often ask myself, "Do I appreciate Calvary like I should? Do I appreciate my gifts? Do I express my appreciation, and is it causing my love to grow?"

Once I was on a plane between Phoenix and Dallas with Billy Graham, whom I've known since he first started work with Youth for Christ. In a break in the conversation, I asked him, "Billy, you've never gotten over the surprise that God picked you, have you?" He replied, "Not only that, Fred, but that God has protected me." Billy not only appreciates the gift, he appreciates the protection to use his gift. I am sure his love for the Lord has grown with his blessings.

Is my passion focused?

Every effective leader is imbued with passion. An accomplishment is often in direct proportion to the amount and intensity of the leader's passion. Passion is contagious for followers. It sustains the leader in difficult times. Passion gives hope.

I like this definition of passion: "Passion is concentrated wisdom with high energy in the pursuit of meaning."

My theologian friend Dr. Ramesh Richard said, "First in life, decide on your passion. What is your first love? If you have multiple passions, you'll be ripped to pieces internally, resulting in a fragmented, random life. If anything other than the Lord Jesus Christ is your first love, you will fall into idolatry." Christ is the focus of passion, insuring integrity of leadership.

The advantages of passion are multiple. It brings purpose, unity, intensity, concentration, assuring accomplishment. It gives intentionality to life. Passion gives depth, keeping us from the shallowness of mediocrity. Our life becomes a welder's torch rather than a grass fire.

Writers have pointed out that men like Aleksandr Solzhenitsyn had an undying passion for truth and principle. Mother Teresa, a passion for the dying. Moody, Spurgeon, and Graham—a passion for souls.

It was Edison's passion that kept him going. Churchill's indomitable passion of will gave the British their war stamina. In leadership, focused passion accomplishes much more than scholarly intellect.

Passion comes from two sources. First, those with an extraordinary passion receive it as a gift, for they were created with the capacity for passion. They can unite the mind and heart and spirit. They have the ability to lose themselves in a cause, to dedicate their life to a single purpose, like Paul saying, "This one thing I do," and again, "I determine not to know anything but Jesus Christ and him crucified."

I was listening to an older writer being interviewed by a younger one when the younger asked, "If you had your life to live over, what would you do?" The older writer said, without hesitation, "I'd find something big enough to give myself to."

The second source of passion is the vision. The clearer the vision, the more focused the passion. If the vision becomes blurred, the passion becomes dissipated and weakened. In an organization where everyone buys into and fully understands the passion and purpose, all effort is unified with high energy. An organization without passion is a car without gasoline, a rocket without fuel. Two organizations may have the same general vision, but the one with the deeper passion will have the greater accomplishment.

Passion does not always express itself the same in each leader. One may be quiet, another effervescent. The evidence is not as important as the presence.

The purpose of our passion, though, must have integrity. I have heard corporate leaders complain that their employees don't have the same dedication to success that they have. When you examine this carefully, you find that the executive's dedication is to his personal success, not the success of the organization. If he is honest with himself, he recognizes his ambition is a personal one; he wants self-satisfaction. In a sense, the employees by not going all-out are doing for themselves the same thing he's doing for himself—they are looking out for their interests, not his.

The apostle Paul, a man of exceptional passion, was willing even to be accursed if the purpose for which he was called was not accomplished. Self-sacrifice is the acid test of our passion.

While passion supplies hope, tenacity, energy, and the like, it also increases vision, for it creates its own reality. It is passion that stimulates the imagination to believe "eye hath not seen nor ear heard, neither has it entered into the heart of man the great things the Lord has for those who love him."

I like the prayer of the old saint: "O Lord, fill my will with fire." He was asking for passion with a receptive, expectant attitude toward God. A pure passion turns the ordinary into the extraordinary.

2

MY FRIEND FENELON

INTEGRITY GROWS WITH PROPER ASSOCIATION. Our friendships not only define us but develop and energize us. I have found a new, profitable companion—François Fenelon, the French mystic of three hundred years ago. He and Oswald Chambers are my daily counsel. They differ in that Oswald Chambers was a teacher expounding principles to a group with each person applying it to himself or herself, while Fenelon was a mentor to an individual and focused on specific situations.

For forty-one years I have read Chambers's *My Utmost for His Highest*. I discovered Fenelon's *The Seeking Heart* a short five years ago. After just a few pages, I was hooked. Fenelon was a contemporary and friend of Jeanne Guyon, and both suffered for their faith—she in prison for ten years and he exiled to oblivion after rising to one of the highest offices in the French court.

I include seven themes of Fenelon's that have been most helpful to me. Other themes of his are woven into the fabric of the rest of this book. With our lives rooted in these immutable principles, we can be like the willow tree, with branches and leaves flexible to the changing winds and the roots stable in the realities of life.

1. Self-love is subtle.

I have a friend who points out how self-love constantly changes to keep from being recognized. It is like the way a virus changes to avoid extermination. For example, self-love can come in the guise of guilt: "How could anyone as good as I do anything that bad?" Or a desire for purity might be evidence of self-love—in our wanting God to make us a showcase example, desiring to sit on the right hand of God. Even the desire to *be* significant, rather than the desire to *do* significant things, can be a form of self-love.

Fenelon says, "Do not listen to the voice that suggests you live for yourself. The voice of self-love is even more powerful than the voice of the serpent." Again, "Self-love brings great anxiety." Or, "You will be tempted to speak out in a humble tone of voice to tell others of your problems. Watch out for this. A humility that is still talkative does not run very deep. When you talk too much, your self-love relieves his sense of shame a little."[1]

Fenelon goes on to say, "Self-love is proud of its spiritual accomplishments. You must lose everything to find God for himself alone. You won't begin to let go of yourself until you have been thrown off a cliff. He takes away to

---

[1]François Fenelon, *The Seeking Heart* (Sargent, Ga.: The Seedsowers, 1992).

give back in a better way." He follows up by saying, "Self-interest and pride cause you to reject the gifts of God, because they do not come in a way that suits your taste. He asks for nothing but death, but you desire nothing but life.

"Selfishly loving yourself shunts the spirit. You put yourself in a straitjacket when you are enclosed in self. When you come out of that prison you experience how immense God is and how he sets his children free. Be humble. Do not trust the old nature."

Fenelon probes deeper: "So to strip self-love of its mask is the most humiliating punishment that can be inflicted. You see that you are no longer as wise, patient, polite, self-possessed, and courageous in sacrificing yourself for others as you had imagined. You are no longer fed by the belief that you need nothing. You no longer think that your greatness and generosity deserve a better name than self-love. However, you are further tormented because you also weep and rage that you have cried at all. What your old nature fears the most is necessary for its destruction."

He further warns: "While on the outside you seem to be only concerned with the glory of God, the unconquered self nature deep within is causing you trouble. I am sure that you want God to be glorified, but you want his glory to be expressed through the testimony that he has made you perfect. Let me tell you that this feeds self-love. It is simply a covetous guise of the self nature."

When I read that, I remembered attending Billy Graham's sixtieth birthday in Charlotte, North Carolina, when dignitaries, both in industry and religion, had lavishly praised him. He stood to acknowledge their remarks and opened by quoting the Scripture, "God will not share his glory with another," and then asked that they not tempt him with their praise even though he appreciated it tremendously. It was a high moment of worship.

Fenelon continues, "The self-love which is the source of your faults is also what hides your faults. Self-love must be rooted out of you so that love can reign within you without opposition. Until you see yourself in God's pure light, you really don't know yourself. There is danger in thinking that you are perfect simply because you understand what it would be like to be perfect. All your beautiful theories do not help you die to yourself. Knowledge nourishes the life of Adam in you because you secretly delight in your revelation. Never trust your own power or your own knowledge."

Oswald Chambers continually repeats that the knowledge of God comes through obedience, not learning.

It's possible for a person to have a head for God but not a heart for God. With our head we intellectually understand—but with our heart we obey. Occasionally I talk to someone who feels so much arrogance about his knowledge of God that I suspect if God wanted to take a vacation, this individual would substitute for him.

2. Suffering is useful.

Fenelon speaks of suffering as God's exercise program, his gymnasium, and I can hear myself complaining to God, "You're getting me muscle-bound."

Here are some excerpts: "Suffering is necessary for all of us. You will be purified by dying to your own desires and will. Let yourself die. You have excellent opportunities for this to happen. Don't waste them." For years I have liked the saying, "Never lose the good from a bad experience."

He goes on: "My God, help us to see Jesus as our model in all suffering. You made him a man of sorrows. Teach us how useful sorrow is."

Fenelon writes, "God never makes you suffer unnecessarily. He intends for your suffering to heal and purify you. The hand of God hurts you as little as it can. The yoke that God gives is easy to bear if you accept it without struggling to escape." The yoke, I believe, is easy and comfortable as long as we pull together with the Lord, but when we try to escape, the yoke becomes more like the bit in the horse's mouth.

Fenelon gives us hope by saying, "When I suffer I can never see an end to my trials and when relief comes I am so suspicious that the suffering is not really over that I hesitate to accept my rest. It seems to me that to accept both good and bad seasons alike is to be truly fruitful. Accept both comfort and correction from the hand of God."

Sometimes we hear people trying to define the difference between God's discipline and God's blessing. I don't believe that we can know, at the time, which is which. Indeed, often as we look back we can see that the discipline was the blessing.

3. One test of relation with God is peace.

Recently I was talking to a disturbed Christian business executive. I suggested that he immediately find a knowledgeable theologian who could help him find the spiritual source of his turmoil. Any Christian without peace needs attention.

Fenelon recommends, "Encourage peace, become deaf to your overactive imagination. Your spinning imagination will harm your health and make your spiritual life very dry. You worry yourself sick for no good reason. Inner peace and the sweet presence of God are chased away by restlessness."

Fenelon also writes, "Peace and comfort are to be found only in simple obedience. Remain at peace, for peace is what God wants for you no matter what is happening. There is in fact a peace of conscience which sinners should enjoy as they are repenting. Suffering should be peaceful and tempered with God's comfort."

Regarding the future: "Live in peace without worrying about the future. Unnecessary worrying and imagining the worst possible scenario will strangle your faith."

Fenelon warns that "there never is peace in resisting God. . . . Allow yourself to be humble. If you are silent and peaceful when humiliating things happen to you, you will grow in grace.

"The point of trusting God is not to do great things that you can feel good about, but to trust God from a place of deep weakness. Here's a way to know if you are actually trusting God with something. You will not think about the matter any longer nor will you feel a lack of peace."

It reminds me of the story of Babe Ruth hitting that famous home run for the sick boy. As he left the ballpark, someone asked him, "What if you had struck out?" With a surprised look, Babe answered, "I never thought about it."

Peace does not mean absence of tumult; it can mean security amid the tumult. When I was a small child in church, I heard a minister tell the story of how a wealthy man wanted a picture of peace. Various artists tried different approaches, from a quiet pastoral scene to moonlit nights on the water, but the artist who won painted a bird's nest in a small tree on the edge of a waterfall.

4. Silence brings blessings.

As I read Fenelon on silence, I was reminded of what Oswald Chambers wrote about thanking God when he "trusts us with silence." Fenelon put great emphasis on the value of silence—not only environmental silence, but silence of the soul, stillness of the heart, and tranquillity of the mind.

Fenelon writes, "Sometimes the annoyances that make you long for solitude are better for producing humility than the most complete solitude could be. Do not seek God as if he were far off in an ivory castle. He is found in the middle of the events of your everyday life.

"Listen to the voice of God in silence. Be willing to accept what he wants to show you. God will show you everything you need to know. Be faithful to come before him in silence. When you hear the still, small voice within, it is time to be silent.

"Try to practice silence as much as general courtesy permits. Silence encourages God's presence, prevents harsh words, and causes you to be less likely to say something you will regret. Silence also helps you put space between you and the world. Out of the silence that you cultivate you will get strength to meet your needs."

Most of us aren't silent often enough. A chief executive officer of a large corporation attended a weekend retreat recently. He told me that his most meaningful experience of the retreat was the exercise of listening to someone for ten minutes—without saying anything. He realized how much he learned in that listening silence.

5. Growth and change are the work of the Cross.

Reading Fenelon made me realize how often I do not deeply understand the familiar. I repeat and hear phrases and clichés without really having the depth of understanding that I need.

Fenelon has helped me to think of the work of the Cross—redemption—as the constant tension of growth and change as the old nature gives way to the new. It is a process that starts with the new birth and ends at the close of our earthly journey, by which time we are, we hope, more mature in the likeness of Christ. I'm reminded of the oft-quoted prayer: "Lord, I'm not what I ought to be and I'm not what I'm going to be, but thank you, Lord, I'm not what I used to be."

Some well-meaning Christians confuse the thorn and the cross. The thorn, to me, is something God puts in our lives that keeps us conscious of our dependence on him. Paul had the thorn; Jacob had the limp. The thorn is a constant reminder, but each day I must make the conscious decision to shoulder the cross and go forward.

Fenelon writes, "Bear your cross. Do you know what this means? Learn to see yourself as you are and accept your weakness until it pleases God to heal you. If you die a little every day of your life, you won't have too much to worry about on your final day."

Then with assurance he says, "You and I are nothing without the cross. I agonize and cry when the cross is working within me, but when it is over I look back in admiration for what God has accomplished. Of course I am then ashamed I bore it so poorly."

6. The focused life is the simple life.

God never complicates what can be done simply. The focused life is the powerful life.

The saints I have read seem to have a unified priority system. They are chiefly single-agenda individuals with purity of purpose. Actually, this is what I look for in business—people who are cause-oriented. Those with double agendas are like those with double-mindedness, against which the Scripture warns. When we focus and screw down the nozzle, we increase the force of the water.

Recently I was discussing decision-making with an investment banker. He had good advice: "Once you decide what you want to do and the strategy that will accomplish it, then decision-making becomes simple. You do the things that advance the strategy and avoid the things that hinder it." If, however, you're unsure or tentative about where you want to go, it is much more difficult to find the right road.

Our hidden agendas can poison the simplicity of a situation. The desire to do a work for God is simple enough, but I greatly complicate it when I add the hidden agenda of wanting to be recognized and appreciated while doing it.

7. Give grace to yourself and others.

I can almost hear Fenelon say, "Lighten up." As a person of a humorous bent, I was intrigued that nowhere in his writing does Fenelon mention specifically a sense of humor. I have always felt that humor is one way we accept our fallibility; in fact, most humor lives between where we are and where we wish we were. However, Fenelon doesn't fail to see the weakness and doesn't suggest excusing the weakness, but he emphasizes the grace, the forgiveness, the mercy. These are much stronger than humor.

One of Fenelon's biographers noted, "He was a pleasant person to be around. He had an admirable presence." I have come to think of him as having the presence of Billy Graham, the optimism of Norman Vincent Peale, and the serving spirit of Mother Teresa, though I am sure Fenelon would rap my knuckles for writing that.

Regarding self, Fenelon writes, "Do not be surprised to find yourself overly sensitive, impatient, proud and self-willed. Realize that this is your natural disposition. Bear with yourself but do not flatter yourself into thinking you are better than you are but wait on God's timing to transform it. Stop at once when your activities become too hurried. Do not be eager, even for good things."

In another letter he writes, "Don't let the compliments you receive from worthy people go to your head. On the other hand, do not let a false humility keep you from accepting God's comfort when he sends it through others."

Wouldn't it be wonderful to say in reply to a compliment, "Your compliment is God's comfort to me"?

About temptation he writes, "Temptation is a necessary part of a Christian's life. Don't be upset by even the most shameful temptation. Look at God and dwell continually in his presence. He will keep your feet from falling."

Here I received some additional help from the theologian Peter Kreeft, who said that temptation becomes a sin only when we mix will with it. For example, when a wrongful thought comes into our mind, it is not sinful until by will we recall the thought or dwell on it.

Fenelon doesn't encourage self-evaluation. I think the apostle Paul took this view by saying that he didn't even judge himself. Fenelon says, "If you need to know you're doing well, you're not walking by faith. Constant evaluation is just a preoccupation with yourself. Constant introspection is itself a distraction. You are afraid to pray poorly but you pray best when you don't even realize you're praying. Continue to walk humbly with God without interruption. If you're shown something that should be corrected, then simply do so without becoming legalistic about it."

Regarding others, Fenelon writes, "The daily standards that you live by should not be relaxed in any way, yet you must deal gently with the faults of others. Learn to be lenient with the less important matters but maintain your firmness over that which is essential. Remember that true firmness is gentle, humble, and calm. A sharp tongue, a proud heart, and an iron hand have no place in God's work. Wisdom sweetly orders all things.

"Stay away from people who sound good but never exhibit true fruit of the inward walk. Their talk is deceptive and you will almost always find them restless, fault-finding and full of their own thoughts. These spiritual busybodies are annoyed with everything and are almost always annoying."

As I read Fenelon, I could almost hear him encouraging the readers of his letters the way Paul encouraged the church: "Follow me as I follow Christ." Run the race with patience and complete the course and your reward will be "Well done, good and faithful servant."

3

WEIGHING CHARACTER

LEADERS WITH STRONG CHARACTER have power, dignity, and integrity. Christian character is built around the divine cardinal virtues. Character develops when the mind and heart instruct the will in accepting these controlling virtues, out of which come Christlike values and actions.

Divine virtues are the roots from which such values grow. The virtues are the principles. The values produce techniques, the modus operandi.

Where the virtues are perverted by Satan, the character is evil. It may be strong or weak, but it is destructive. In this chapter, I will deal mainly with the development and evidence of good character—the foundation on which to build a life of respect and worth.

Fortunately our character can be strong without being perfect. Christ alone had perfect character. David, the man after God's own heart, had faults. Peter, the disciple of Jesus, could be fickle. Moses, strong-willed and yet afraid. Abraham could lie. Bold Elijah became scared. These, and many others in Scripture, had strong character, though not perfect.

When I was young I often heard the cliché "God can use any vessel except a dirty one." From my many years in Christian work, however, I found that God does use dirty ones, because he doesn't have any other kind to use. All of God's children have flawed character. Those who appear flawless have not been pressured enough in their vulnerable spot.

It is enough that we *want* solid character, for then we are teachable and reclaimable after failing. The worst flaw is to believe we are not vulnerable. We must always pray, "Lord, lead us not into temptation," and when in temptation must believe that he has provided a way of escape.

It is helpful to know our weak points: the ego, fear to confront, love or envy of money, peer pressure, sex, or private obsession. The Scripture tells us not to make a vow to God that we won't keep. Vow failure is a character matter.

Evaluating others

It would be helpful if we could have a load-limit sign on our character, like that on a bridge. One of my preacher friends was coming under the influence of a man of extensive wealth. As the man plied my friend with benefits, this wealthy person began to ask questionable favors. My friend broke the relation, saying to him, "I'm afraid I have a price, and you're getting too close to it."

Personality has an effect on character, for it fosters different pressures and desires. I know a talented, wealthy young executive who is exceptionally introverted. Occasionally he talks to me about the pressures of being an introvert and his desire to change. But his introversion protects his strong desire to be right. I have rarely met a man who wanted to be right as much as he. His introversion protects against an overwhelming desire to be liked, to be the first to talk, to lead. A situation must build pressure to bring him out. He does his homework. He synthesizes the aspects of an issue, permitting him to be in the limelight as little as possible. He must be drawn out, while most extroverts must be reined in, either by self or others.

As a leader, a friend, or a counselor, I have tried to validate the areas of health or weakness in the character of those with whom I share responsibility. I have sometimes been criticized by my associates for going to what they feel are extreme lengths to ascertain weakness and strength in a person's character. I do it for a definite reason—I don't want to be surprised. I want to know the person so I can build on his strength and buttress his weakness. Since character is the foundation of relation and accomplishment, I don't apologize for evaluating someone's strengths and weaknesses. I prefer to test someone when failure is not fatal. Marines build character that will stand up under fire. They don't want failure when it counts most. To "give others the benefit of the doubt" sounds good, but that isn't good stewardship in leadership. Napoleon said that the most dangerous general was one who fought based on fantasy. So it is with a person trying to lead based on fantasy or ignorance of the character of his or her associates.

In evaluating character, I start with the known past. Few people change character after becoming an adult. I not only quiz the person but also everyone who might be knowledgeable about him or her, particularly the spouse. Our family and close friends know our character much better than our talents.

Another good method is to tell stories that get a reflex reaction. For example, a salesperson will laugh when another salesperson outwits a tough customer, but a doctor doesn't laugh when another doctor takes advantage of a patient. The ethics of the doctor will typically be higher regarding the patient than those of the salesperson regarding the customer. However, the doctor might guffaw at a story about beating the government out of taxes. Stories reveal the heart. People become involved in stories.

Humor draws out spontaneous reaction, which is a window into character. In the past I've spoken many times in Las Vegas at conventions and while there heard famous comedians. Inevitably they test the edge of social acceptance, even in such matters as ridiculing religion and God. Listen to the audience's reaction, and you have a fair evaluation of the character of a person or a crowd.

Evaluating our own character

In evaluating our character, we will be better judges of matters not directly involving our personal welfare. This is the basis of America's jury system. Uninvolved individuals tend to be more open-minded and, we hope, fair-minded.

That is one reason to have a qualified person to help make decisions when we are personally involved. We tend to feel any proposition that favors us is fair. We want the machine slightly tilted in our direction. We deserve it—or at least we can rationalize that we do.

Once I was on a corporate board whose director wanted his son elevated above what most of us felt was his capability. His father, normally a fair-minded, objective executive, lost reason in his campaign for his son. I would rather have sold refrigerators to Eskimos than try to convince this father his son wasn't the one deserving promotion.

I have found that an outside "authority figure" is most helpful in difficult decisions that involve my character. I use several authority figures, for I want an expert in the area of the counsel I'm seeking. One has impeccable social sense, another financial fairness, and others have further areas of expertise. It is possible they would ask my opinion on the same matter if they were involved. The critical point is the difference personal involvement makes. The ultimate question in evaluating our own character is, Do I really, truly want to be right? Do I believe right is best?

One of the surest evidences of fine character is its clarity. Pure character is transparent. We say, "You can see right through the person" or "What you see is what you get" or "He is all wool and a yard wide." My favorite signature is the one Jeb Stuart used in signing his letters to his commander, Robert E. Lee: "Yours to count on." When I wrote notes to my mentor, Maxey Jarman, I signed them YTCO. He understood, for he had given me the story.

A few years back, I was leading a seminar on speaking, which was attended by many ministers. I had used various illustrations, mostly from my own experience. One of the ministers said that he envied my exciting life because I had a lot of stories to tell. Another minister told him, "You've got the same kind of stories, but you don't want to tell them because you don't want people to see you."

Clarity can be clouded by self-serving confessions. One doesn't have to be astute to recognize when a speaker is hitting two licks for himself while hitting one for God. Self-serving confession is one of the tools used most often. For example, a young speaker said, "While I was valedictorian of my high school class as well as my college class and one of the youngest men to ever receive a Ph.D., I realize that God knows more than I do, and I have to be humble in his presence." I blush to think how many times I have done that. I'm instructed by the verse, "As a dog returns to his vomit, so a fool returns to his foolishness." Every time I do it I wonder, *Why can't I just hit licks for God and forget myself?*

The seventeenth-century Christian writer Michael Molinos said, "You are willing to say things about yourself to disclose your faults before others and many other such impressive things, but within you, you are justifying yourself far more than you are seeing your faults. By such means the monster within you returns again and again to esteem himself." One way we can tell if we're self-serving is when we are tempted to augment what we say according to the audience reaction. I find confession easily turns into explanation and then into justification, or at least rationalization.

Christians should not be concerned with image but with worth. The more I appreciate my worth in Christ, the less I care about my image. Our infatuation with image causes a lot of the alienation in society. We are afraid to let people get close to us for fear they will see that the image is really a mask. Our son Fred was visiting with a preacher who originally got a lot of recognition for his creativity;

then he decided to focus his ministry on a few square blocks in his city. Fred took his young daughter to meet him, wanting her to know people of real substance. After reviewing what he was doing, Fred said to him, "With publicity you could become famous." To which the minister replied, "And shallow."

Character is tested in commitment. We worship a God who commits, who covenants. The strength to commit is in character. In 2 Samuel, Ittai committed to David. When David gave him an out to join the opposition with Absalom, he said, in effect, "I came to stay." When Naomi asked Ruth if she would leave, she said, "I came to stay."

Years ago I read a story of a pastor struggling with a small church on the frontier, eking out a living for his growing family, yet devoted to his small flock. One day an opportunity arose for him to go to a bigger church that would provide better for his family. He announced his departure, and on the day they loaded up the wagon to leave, the townsfolk gathered around, crying to see them go. As they started to leave, he suddenly pulled up the horses, the family got out of the wagon, and they started hugging their friends and unloading the furniture. They had decided to stay.

Tongue control is another character issue, illustrated by the book of James. When I was a young man, I led singing for revivals in the South. I was never a good musician, but I could wave my arms enthusiastically, remembering that Billy Sunday got Homer Rodeheaver to lead singing not because he was the best musician but because he was the best cheerleader in school. A small church in an outlying suburb was without a music director, and the pastor invited me to lead singing on a temporary basis. When I agreed to come, he had a serious talk with me and asked me to promise him that I would never say a negative thing about anybody in the congregation. This was a difficult promise for me, but I kept it, and I've never felt such freedom with people in my life.

Since I knew I had never said anything negative about anyone there, I could be perfectly free in conversation, without any veil of guilt. It was a lesson I wish I would have applied in other situations.

Obedience builds character. Fortunately, character can be strengthened just the same as habits and reflexes can be developed. First, there must be the desire, then there must be the repetition over a long enough period for it to form into a habit. When the habit is practiced it develops into a reflex. Frank Laubach wrote of how his thinking of God constantly started out laboriously but as it developed, it became easier and easier until at last it became natural. That is how aspects of character are developed.

Confession clears or cleans our character. Theologically, we speak of the "washing of the blood." In confession we bring ourselves to this fountain, this source of cleansing.

Instead of confession, often we see leaders put a spin on sin. Before we got the modern term *spin*, we called it "rationalization." When the prophet Nathan confronted King David, David didn't run for the spin doctors. He had the character to confess and to accept forgiveness—and to take the consequences. He wasn't like the chicken thief down South who when confronted by the judge replied, "Guilty, and waive the hearing," to which the judge asked,

"What do you mean, 'waive the hearing'?"

He replied, "I done it, and I don't want to hear any more about it." David did not turn against God when he had to suffer the consequences of his sin even though he was forgiven.

Character grows strong under pressure, suffering, loss, tribulation, and failures, in which the mind gets experiences and the heart gets convictions. Character is the element that makes us stand when we want to run, to live when it would be easier to die, to fight for right in a losing cause, saying with Abraham Lincoln, "I'd rather fail in a cause that will ultimately succeed than succeed in a cause that will ultimately fail."

Disciplined decisions

As leaders, our decisions determine the character of our organizations. We cannot afford to make exceptions for ourselves. If the president takes company material for personal use, that excuses others. In fact, a little dishonesty at the top encourages much more at the bottom. Dishonest handling of expenses, for example, is inexcusable. I have seen some leaders overlook or excuse "small dishonesties" as a way to glue the organization to the leader through guilt. They may even call this "perks."

The leader is responsible for keeping options in line with right character. If honesty is the best policy, then it must be the only policy. At Genesco, where I worked as an executive, the president was firm in saying, "If it has to be done, then it can be done right. If it can't be done right, it doesn't have to be done." This pressured us to come up with creative options to accomplish what needed to be done when others took shortcuts.

Character decisions must be disciplined decisions. Decisions made for any of the following reasons invariably prevent leaders from building character in an organization.

1. *Trying to maintain control.* It is the natural tendency of leadership to protect its position. Such leadership structures the organization for personal control, not for leadership development. This might be acceptable in corporations, but not in Christian work. Once I was involved in a ministry reorganization that raised the control question: "Is this work his or His?" Did it belong to the leader or to God?

I have heard leaders say, "God called me to lead this organization," and I wanted to ask, "For what purpose? That you might have a lifetime job, or that the mission of the organization might be best accomplished?"

Generally a leader who is control-driven is serving self more than God. This desire for control is a major character issue. There are times in emergencies when unified control is necessary for survival, similar to giving the president "wartime powers," but only in emergencies, not as a way of leadership.

Dictators do not develop strong leaders for succession. Once I was asked if I'd be interested in becoming president of a manufacturing corporation that had a long-term dictatorial leader who had recently died. I knew my team approach would not be profitable, for the subordinates had been taught to act on orders, not to think through solutions. I couldn't in good conscience ask people who hadn't taken responsibility for results for years to begin to think for themselves. The corporation needed a younger dictator to keep the company successful.

Recently a long-term pastor told me how difficult it is for a new pastor to follow one with a long service history. When the old pastor is even a quasi dictator, it becomes impossible for the first or second new pastor after him to succeed. Usually by the time the third pastor comes along, he is able to change the system to fit his style.

Historically, a benevolent dictator with great ability is the most efficient leader for most organizations over the time of his service. Long term, however, he is frequently a detriment to the health of the organization after he leaves.

In corporate management I was taught that the perpetuity of the healthy organization is management's first responsibility, and so leadership development at all levels is of prime importance. Successful succession is a leader's responsibility and often a test of his character.

2. *Trying to outdo the competition.* Another pitfall for good character decisions is "competitiveness." I believe in healthy competition in business and athletics, but not in spiritual service. We Baptists joke about our pattern of growth, which is to fight, split, and compete, all the time talking of how God is blessing us as we outdo our competition.

The parachurch movement would never have grown so large if Christian denominations could cooperate rather than compete. Today, with the proliferation of parachurch ministries, every function other than funerals, weddings, and baptisms can be done with the parachurch emphasis. The church retains the ritual while the parachurch siphons off much vital leadership and financial support.

Now, as always, evangelism, spiritual discipline, Bible study, and financial support are normal functions of the established church. But the parachurch brought changes in methodology that the church was reluctant to accept. In some places, churches are beginning to adapt. The church can learn much from the parachurch movement. Cooperation is a character decision that can be marred by competition between leaders and organizations. There is one situation in which all Christians would be happy to work together—persecution. Sometimes I think we are tempting God to send persecution just to let us experience our oneness in him.

While I have found much to differ on with the brilliant Harvard professor Dr. Harvey Cox, I wholeheartedly agree with his observation: "Christ united the church and man divided it." I wish I could believe all differences among religious leaders were an effort to purify the faith, but I would have to check my intellectual integrity at the door to believe it. Most strong leaders have strong egos, and ego satisfaction is a character fault in Christian work.

It is always good to remind myself that Christian leadership is flawed. Some flaws show more than others and in different ways. After reading Oswald Chambers, I try not to be surprised at sin in any of its forms—disappointed, yes; surprised, no.

Once I was playing golf with a well-known Christian leader. Riding together as partners, we came to his ball and found it fairly deep in the rough. He looked across the fairway and saw that the others were not looking, so he kicked his ball out to the edge of the fairway. Shortly before that, he had been lecturing me about the inerrancy of Scripture, fearing I was not thrilled with the divisions the argument was causing. Seeing him kick his ball out of the rough weakened his theological authenticity.

3. *Refusing to admit mistakes.* A friend went through a terrible experience when he served on a board that allowed itself to be bullied out of holding an honest position. The financial pressure became too great. Repeatedly some of the board members would surreptitiously bring up the possibility of reversing an action they had taken, without stirring the hostility of the opposition. My friend asked, "Why don't we just say that we were wrong and acted hastily without proper consideration, and now we're going to reverse our decision?"

He said, "That sent them into fits of denial."

In finances we learn to take a loss as soon as possible—cut the loss, don't throw good money after bad; only obsessive gamblers do that. By the same logic, leaders must name and claim mistakes as soon as possible. Minimize the loss, and start remedial actions immediately.

4. *Protecting an individual at the expense of the organization.* Another area of Christian character applies to "references." I have found asking for character references among the Christian community to be useless. Too often we rationalize our tolerance and compassion or our fear of making enemies. Why not tell the truth? If we know a person has character flaws, why not protect the organization that is inquiring? If we prefer not to talk, then say so. Character requires that we not give someone a reference he or she does not deserve.

5. *Hiring or promoting people based on politics.* Generally we see a person's strengths first and experience his or her

weaknesses later. Hiring and promoting with integrity means acting according to record and gifts, not according to politics, relations, or influence.

A leader's first question should be, "How will this appointment help the organization to fulfill its mission?" not "Will the person vote my way?"

6. *Playing loose with the truth.* I originally listed "lying" as one of the flaws in character decision-making. However, I know few Christian leaders who actually intend to lie. Once I was speaking at the Billy Graham Center in Wheaton to a large group of ministers. I asked them why, on a Monday morning at one of their ministerial meetings, they were not more truthful with each other. It seemed that all who spoke were claiming the blessing of God and a great outpouring of the Spirit. As I got to know some of these men, some were struggling to maintain their zeal and balance. At the close of the session, a young pastor of a small church chided me by saying, "Fred, you're suggesting we commit professional suicide. If we told each other the truth, we'd be dead."

Another twisting of the truth is when a preacher says, "God told me" as persuasion. Leaders must have integrity of vocabulary, including avoiding pious babble not understood by nonbelievers and not believed by many believers. In my long experience with Christian organizations, I have seen too many "special visions from God" play out in less than divine ways. Some have failed miserably. One business executive publicly bragged that God ran his business, and later it went into bankruptcy. I think such leaders are basically sincere, but rather than hearing God's voice, they hear an echo of their own desire voiced to God. Most of the time I have found that God's will comes in an orderly fashion, in circumstances evidenced by several praying individuals.

I asked a great man of God from the East how Christians in that part of the world determine God's will. He said, "The first who has the impression shares it with others. We pray and watch circumstances. If favorable circumstances start to coalesce, we pray more and wait until we are unified in spirit. Then we start, knowing that if it is not his will, he will impress us to stop it. We remain open to stop."

There is real mysticism in this but no magic. The eternal God does not have to have everything done during our administration. Maybe we should build a foundation and others the superstructure, while still others finish the job. One plants, another waters, another reaps, and God gets the glory.

The person of God needs integrity of character—not perfect character, but strong enough to build and lead an organization with integrity and honesty of purpose.

4

STAYING WITH YOUR CALL

RECENTLY I ATTENDED A WIDELY ADVERTISED, elite conference for Christian leaders preparing for the future. It was well presented, well attended, and impressive. When they asked for my evaluation, I pointed out that the material presented was the same material I had presented years before in speaking to the presidents' conference of the American Management Association. It was good management and leadership methodology but not spiritual.

No one at that conference discussed maintaining the spiritual vitality of the leader, the most important element in Christian leadership. The new methodology does not depend on the presence of the Holy Spirit but upon research and human leadership.

The church is a spiritual organization, not a human one. Human methods work in business but eventually drain the power and effectiveness of a spiritual endeavor. Human methods can grow a church, build an impressive facility, create exciting programs, and develop strong leadership, but not spiritual leadership.

If we define the church's success by human criteria, then human methods work, and work well. However, if the church's success is measured by new birth, not new members; by maturity, not activity; and by fellowship, not by member entertainment, then scriptural leadership is necessary. God is as interested in the method as he is in the results.

Human methods assume Christian leaders are ranchers, not shepherds. But those called to be shepherds are not equipped by gift or ambition to be ranchers. The danger is that the call will turn into a profession, that the spiritual leader will possess the same motivation, personality, and skills that the corporate executive does.

Human leadership is motivated by power, prestige, and money (including perks). The system is set up to provide these, which are not the motivations of a spiritual leader. Most pastors do not have the ambition, competitiveness, or toughness of most CEOs, and their master is the Lord, not a board of directors or stockholders. I have spent many years in American industry, both as an officer and a board member, as well as serving many years as chairman of several national ministries. The purpose of the corporation and the purpose of the church are very different. The church is not a corporation. The church exists for relationship with God and other believers, not for profit. It is more a living organism than an organization. The members are not employees to be hired and fired based on their efficiency.

Let me define power, prestige, and money as motivation: the power to perpetuate the leader's control as well as the life of the organization; to institute programs and procedures and see that they succeed, penalizing those who fail; to arrange people by results and reward loyalty; to combine with others in mergers or acquisitions; to influence one's successor and, ultimately, to control one's personal destiny.

In prestige this type of leader gets recognition, respect—for himself and his organization. This person is catered to, often attaining celebrity status. Prestige gives him social and political inclusion among the elite. He can join the best clubs, be elected to positions of power, honor, and influence. With financial reward he finds security as well as "the good life," meaning comfort and often luxury, which often rewards such a leader much more than he deserves because he, in reality, controls the system.

Power, prestige, and money appeal to most of us, and to use methods that produce these will continue to be a temptation. I have seen spiritual leaders seduced into leaving their calling and becoming professionals in the American religious industry, which utilizes these same motivations and rewards. Unfortunately, they become ambitious, egotistical, metallic, and remote, only interested in people who advance their agenda. Self-love has taken over.

Those promoting this methodology predict dire results for those who stay with "old-fashioned, out-dated" methods. Others predict that only the megachurch will survive—that small churches may not be viable. But I think history shows small flocks will always be effective. The church's basic functions have been and will be the salvation of the lost, the maturing of the saved, and the fellowship that encourages Christian living. This can be done in a small group as well as in a large one. The church still faces, no matter its size, two basic questions: Can Christ be Savior without being Lord? and Are members customers or distributors? The church of any size is faced with the temptation to make the irresponsible comfortable.

Spiritual leadership

In business I was taught not to criticize anything without having something better to recommend. Therefore I felt frustrated in criticizing those Christian leaders who I felt had forfeited their calling for a professional position. I'm not enough of a theologian to do an exhaustive Bible study defining spiritual leadership. Nor can I be happy coming up with a theoretical definition based on my own opinion.

As I wrestled with this problem, I suddenly thought of spiritual leaders I have known and their common denominators. I made a list of the outstanding qualities of three specific men, out of the many I have known, who are leading successful ministries (accomplishing their goals). These three with whom I have worked for years personify to me spiritual leadership.

These three would not remind you of each other if you met them separately. They are not cookie-cutter characters. They obviously have accepted their uniqueness and are not trying to portray an accepted image. I am positive, however, that if they met together, there would be instant harmony and absolutely no competitiveness. You'd be impressed by each one's confidence yet genuine humility. They don't talk humbly, they are humble. They have no hint of false humility. Their confidence is in their calling. When God calls, he equips with gifts and opportunities.

Each is highly intelligent; two won high academic honors, and I'm not sure about the academic achievements of the third. They have an intellectual curiosity that keeps them current yet a wisdom born of scriptural principles that keeps them wise. They do not look on their intelligence as a separation between themselves and others. Rather, they use it to serve others. Like a doctor who uses his health to serve the sick, so they use their intelligence and wisdom to serve the less knowledgeable.

All have a keen sense of personal relationship with God, both in doing his will and ultimately in being judged by him. Their goal is to hear "Well done, good and profitable servant." Like the servants in the parable, they expect God to ask them about their profitability to him, not their personal enjoyment or celebrity status. (On the contrary, leaders seduced by power, prestige, and money may hear the Lord say, "You got your reward on earth. There is very little left for you up here.") Their self-love has been lost in the cause of Christ.

These spiritual leaders seemingly delight in anonymity. They don't seek honors or take time to do activities just for recognition. They, like Mother Teresa, would rather work than be honored. They quickly give any honor or recognition to others. Anonymity contributes to Christian solitude and meditation. Focus is a great time-saver.

Their vision is accreted, not impetuously arrived at by some special "three A.M. revelation" from God himself. They understand the power of genuine consensus and participation in a shared vision that all accept as having come from God. They never mandate vision on their organizations.

Each organization is exceptionally lean. Administration is a necessary evil and must be done as efficiently as possible in order to minimize the time and energy devoted to it. These spiritual leaders select associates according to gifts and passion, knowing that work delegated to people with the proper gifts and passion needs little supervision, only coordination to move the vision forward. None of them is cursed with the need to be needed. They are anxious for others to get the credit.

Each defines the intended accomplishment of the organization very specifically. It may be to change thinking, develop attitudes, influence behavior, or accomplish a specific mission. No matter what the organization is doing, it is well disciplined in getting defined results. These leaders are not interested in maintaining a program. If there's no wheat coming out of the thresher, they shut it off. I have been impressed at how quickly they stop nonproductive activity.

Each is a creative thinker. Their minds range outside of the box. Knowing what they are trying to accomplish, they are able to see the opportunities as well as the problems.

Each has an unmistakable freshness to his life, as if the Spirit is continually pouring power into him. They have a deep peace, with no continual judging of themselves about whether they are doing what they ought to do or succeeding as they ought to succeed. There seems to be a deep spring of joy in their lives, and though they laugh very differently, they all laugh easily. They seem to have no image to protect and therefore are able to be personable on a one-on-one basis.

Something good today

Let me tell you a story I told two of these spiritual leaders:

Several years ago I had a major operation in the Methodist hospital in Rochester, Minnesota. My wife said she felt sorry for the doctors and hospital staff because she knew how executive I could be, meaning "how controlling I could be." She knew I'd quiz the doctors about their qualifications, as pleasantly as possible, but as thoroughly as possible. For example, I had found out that the surgeon who was to operate on me had been on vacation, so I asked him to make me his second operation that day; I wanted him to get his hand back in the swing of things before he cut me. He laughed, and actually complied.

Then my wife knew I would put my management eye on the hospital, asking why they did what they did and why they arranged things the way they did, hoping to make some improvement. I was to be in the hospital a week, which would give me lots of supervising time.

But something happened that changed all that.

As I sat in the waiting room to be admitted, I was paged to the counter and asked to put all my valuables in a safety deposit box for the duration of my stay. As I put my watch, wallet, and other valuables in, it suddenly occurred to me that my ego was the asset I most valued, and I decided I would put it in the box with the other valuables. That meant I had to be totally submissive to the doctors and nurses, and cooperate with anything they asked. I kept my resolve for the entire week and never had a more enjoyable week in my life. I never knew what a relief it could be not to be establishing the pecking order with people, not to be focusing on the differences but the similarities. I found the joy of community rather than the responsibility of leadership.

Many nights I was awake, and the nurses would visit me. Other times I listened to the radio, both classical and jazz. Late one night the program was recordings of Bix Biederbeck, and the disc jockey read off the side men, including Bill Rank on trombone. It brought back a wonderful memory of finding that Bill Rank worked for me on the night shift in the plant after Dixieland jazz had lost its marketability. I remember talking to Bill about his time playing with Bix and encouraged him to get back into music. With the return of the popularity of Dixieland, he did just that.

The point of the story is that in the middle of the night, one of the nurses came in and said, "I'm going to ask something of you that I've never asked of another patient in my life." When I nodded agreement, she said, "Down the hall we have a young woman who is dying, without a single flower in her room. You have nineteen arrangements. Could I take one to her? She is a black girl without anyone with her."

I pointed to a beautiful arrangement made up of exotic flowers from Hawaii, sent to me by the Highland Park Presbyterian Church. In the middle was a beautiful bird of paradise. I suggested she take that. About thirty minutes later, the nurse came in choked with emotion and started walking around the room. She walked to the foot of my bed and squeezed my big toe and left the room. She was essentially saying, "Tonight we did something good." I can never forget that feeling. Sometimes when I'm not sleeping at night, I wish the Lord would squeeze my toe and say, "We did something good today."

The spiritual leaders whom I write about identified with that story. "We did something good today" is their heart's desire.

I'm sure if I let all three leaders read this, they would not identify themselves in this chapter. They may see in it something of what they believe they try to do, but they would not be egotistical enough to think of themselves as spiritual leaders. Spirituality is somewhat like wisdom. If you think you're wise, you're not. As Oswald Chambers said, "To be spiritual by effort is a sure sign of a false relation with God."

A flexibility born of faith

As I think about spiritual leadership, I become convinced that the key is the Holy Spirit energizing and directing the leader's uniqueness and gifts by giving him or her a vision that creates a passion. I have never known a lazy or confused leader who had a clear sense of passion.

For twenty years I've been writing for Christian leaders. I've spoken to many groups, both large and small. I realize that it is a difficult time to be a Christian spiritual leader in an almost totally secular society whose great renewed interest in spirituality is cultish, not Christian. Christian leaders have lost much of the respect they once had in society. Burnout is common. Depression is almost epidemic. And stress seems to be growing. Immorality and divorce seem to be increasing. Short tenure is becoming too common. More and more preachers and teachers are faced with the demand for entertainment in their message and excitement in their programs.

Could a major part of the problem be that leaders have lost their vital identification with the Lord? Have they become convinced they work for the church rather than for God? Those who feel they work for a church board surrender their authority in spiritual leadership.

I believe there is a flexibility in spiritual leadership that is based on faith in God's provision and direction. It is a calling, not a career. I have great respect for a prominent minister who privately says, "I would be glad to get out of the ministry if God would let me off the hook. In fact, if he doesn't keep me in it, I want out of it."

It is possible, even probable, that some in Christian leadership are misplaced. Leaders who are not endowed with gifts energized by the Spirit become easy prey to the human methodology of leadership. This opens them to the temptation of power, prestige, and money. The three individuals I have been discussing never show any signs of insecurity in what they do. They seem to have the flexibility born of faith. They didn't manipulate their way into leadership, nor are they going to manipulate their staying there. They have a calling to fulfill, not a profession to pursue. Each has a strong feeling of stewardship but little feeling of ownership. They are great by serving. They know joy!

True to the end

My father stayed with his calling to the end. On June 1, 1959, between 12:50 and 3:15 A.M., I sat with my father's corpse and wrote a tribute to him for a friend who didn't know him:

I find myself unconsciously telling you about my father.

He never owned a home or a share of stock. His estate is $1,000 of life insurance. His salary range for life was from $125 to $300 per month. On this he raised five sons after tithing the gross plus a generous "gift" above the tithe, along with charity to all who asked. If he had two suits, he looked for someone who needed one. He never graduated from college or held a degree. There were no honors significant enough to mention in his obituary. He never held an office of any responsibility within his profession. Dad walked the slums like a padre, carrying home the drunks, feeding the bums until Mother hid the food, visiting convicts, riding ambulances with fighting and feuding families, visiting the sick, marrying lovers, and burying the dead.

When his neighbors were hungry, he couldn't eat. When they were sad, he cried, and when they laughed, he out-laughed them.

Through the funeral parlor poured people of all stations and status—the poor, those energized by poverty to move out and up, from the wealthy president whom Father saw converted from a young infidel in a charity TB hospital to the widow who asked to sit alone with him and to relive his great comfort in her past sorrows. In the line were the reclaimed of the rough stuff of life, recounting their experiences with him, and those who felt his great Irish temper he self-indulgently termed "righteous indignation." They all came and sat for hours. No tears were there . . . just victory. Vicariously they felt victorious over death. Because he lived, they knew heaven exists. Where else could he be? A spirit so big could not vanish.

Because he was there they felt a friend at court awaiting them. The atmosphere of triumph was great and positive. No generated hysterical quality. No tears to appease any guilt. Only love, returned to one who truly loved, loved so much that it could be described only as a gift like a talent.

Yes, I realized how great the artist of love was who had shown them the result and not the labor. I knew how often his soul was tired, how many nights he prayed to keep from quitting, how he struggled for thirty-five years in and out of debt to feed his family, how he suffered because he couldn't contribute to his children's education. But there were prayer and encouragement aplenty. The family separately and unanimously decided our greatest witness to his life could be expressed by the absence of grief. If we believed the "blessed hope" he preached, we certainly needed to express it now. Temporary separation, yes—permanent, no.

Late tonight he and I were alone for the last

time. I felt he was asleep. He must be asleep or we would be matching wits. I can't remember when that started, and it never ended. He was never awake but what we were debating, his hobby and greatest achievement in school. It was my honor to be chosen his permanent adversary, even though it might have kept our personal relations in a defensive position. We neither asked nor gave quarter, or conceded defeat.

As he slept in his casket, I studied the mammoth right arm of a former blacksmith who could throw a horse and muscle out two large sledgehammers, holding each by the end of its long handle. Outstretched, his arms, like giant tree limbs, could hold his entire family of five sons, arms so large and powerful that a visitor to the hospital asked if they were swollen even though he was past seventy.

His hands were more expressive than his arms. Somehow they were more personal to me. There was the strong right hand of sudden justice, which literally broke tree limbs over my back for real or imagined breaches of parental law. His ring was off—the telltale gold initial ring that told me there was no Santa Claus when he was dressed up to play the part. Hands that were large and strong to slap me backwards or to gently break the bread of life at the Communion table. Hands that gripped a baseball and turned it loose as fast as any I've ever caught. Hands that pushed the door to avoid any privacy for fear of evil. Hands that helped everyone in need. To see them folded seemed unnatural. They should have been turned out to others.

Pale and spent, his face showed the long battle of death. His great desire to be lucid in death was denied him. He wanted to die describing to his family the glories of the heavens he had "lost his life to save" for eternity. He wanted to prove the rightness of his faith, yet his family must believe as he did, accepting Christ as the bridge between life and death—man and God. This we do.

He was not a brilliant intellect or a gifted orator. However, as an artist of love he was possessed by the living presence of his Savior Jesus Christ whose Second Coming was his most ardent wish. At the funeral we bury his problem (his body), not his greatness (his soul). Crowds will come, as to the funeral of any great man; the big difference will be in the direction of their thoughts. They will be thinking of the Master of the man, not of the mastery of the man. His life and death pointed the same way, up toward God and eternity.

And now he is among that "great cloud of witnesses" who watch us run this mortal race. "Therefore let us lay aside the weight of sin that doth so easily beset us, and let us run with patience the race that is set before us, looking unto Jesus, the author and finisher of our faith." Many have joined that cloud because of him. Many more will ride ashore on the expanding ripples of his life. "O Death, where is thy sting? O Grave, where is thy victory?" He now knows the truth of reality.

5

ESSAYS ON CHRISTIAN CHARACTER

THE DANGERS OF POPULARITY

Christian leaders should never base their leadership on their popularity or saintliness. Those who do, risk damaging the faith of their followers in the event the leaders fall morally. A church leader who as the ruling elder had baptized some of the children of the church divorced his wife and married his secretary. Some of the parents wanted their children rebaptized because they felt the baptisms were invalidated by his behavior.

Oswald Chambers warns us to beware of the temptation to stay between God and the person we are leading. He points out that as soon as the person sees Christ, we should get out of the way. Our cause is Christ.

VALUES OR VIRTUES?

Unless our values are rooted in scriptural virtues, they are not Christian. Our need is not to return to family values or historical values but to scriptural virtues.

We talk about *values* because subconsciously we like to be in control; *we* set our values. Virtues, however, hold their authority because they are not under human control but come from revealed truth. Our society could return to the values of our forefathers, and we could still have human values.

When we return to virtue, we return to God.

THE POWER OF FLATTERY

Flattery subtly used has immense power.

While addressing a large group of supporters for a Christian college, I said that one gift of some leaders of large Christian organizations is their ability to make the irresponsible comfortable. How else, I said, could large Christian organizations be as ineffective as they are? As an example, I pointed out that some of the largest churches in this country are larger than all the early church was, except they aren't turning their city upside down, much less the country.

I tried not to be meanspirited, using my criticism as medicine for a disease rather than a dagger for destruction. Scripture says, "Faithful are the wounds of a friend."

A popular minister immediately followed me and removed the sting by flattering the assembly. He indicated that they were the kind of people the world needs and if everyone were as good as they, there would be no problems. When he got through talking about the "dear, sweet people," I understood for the first time the power of subtle flattery.

THE POWER OF PASSION

Respected church consultant Lyle Schaller has said that if a pastor does not have a passion for the mission, he can forget the rest of leadership. A passion to make a worthwhile difference is indispensable to effectiveness. Passion and vision need to work together. Passion energizes vision, and vision disciplines the passion. The clearer the vision, the greater the passion. The closer we get to the goal, the more it demands of us and the more it means to us.

THE PROPER USE OF POWER

Power comes in many forms. It can be coercive or constructive. Power is necessary to get things done. It is the gasoline for the engine. Power can be used negatively to induce fear or positively as an affirming influence. There is both human power and spiritual power. Either can be used correctly or abused. Our character determines our use of power.

Here are a few examples of power a leader may use:

- The power of responsibility—conferred by authority or title.
- The power of persuasion—the ability to move an organization.
- The power of a charismatic personality—which can unite an effort.
- The power of a great vision (e.g., George Mueller's vision for the care of orphans).
- The power of verbalization—the ability to express an idea in simple terms so people are moved to act.

Power correctly used is always a means and never an end.

PICKING THE RIGHT ENEMY

Great leaders have known the power of uniting against a common enemy. The enemy must be defined vividly, urgently, and must be current. America was united against Russian communism. Ever since the collapse of the USSR, the United States has been casting about for a new unifying enemy, with limited success.

Christian leaders are fortunate in having a common enemy, but too often we direct our shots not in his direction but toward others. Our eternal enemy is Satan, but he, like some of our political leaders, is a great spinmaster and gets us to perceive other believers as the Enemy. If he has a sense of diabolical humor, he must be laughing while we wound each other.

ANSWERING THE WRONG QUESTION

I often hear people question the goodness of God by saying, "How could a loving God let my dear one die of cancer?" But disease came as a result of the Fall, not the callousness of God. The question is "What evil did we bring on ourselves when Adam and Eve sinned?"

Too seldom do I hear Satan blamed. He has become the practitioner of transference, ascribing to God his nefarious activities.

BEWARE OF THE CELEBRITY SYNDROME

The celebrity syndrome is one of the ruling principles of our present society. It isn't so much what you are known for as it is that you are well known. Moral tramps sell more books than saints.

Our son Fred invited a Christian layman who was experiencing a phenomenal rise in popularity to attend a meeting Fred was holding for laypeople. This Christian leader accepted. A friend of the man remarked to Fred, "You know he will expect to speak."

Fred had not put out the program, and before he did Fred called the assistant of this Christian layman, asking if he expected to speak. The assistant said, "Nothing could be further from the truth. He doesn't want to speak. He just wants to attend."

The experience was so unusual, Fred called his entire staff together and told them, "We have found a real one," meaning, "a humble one who has not yet accepted the celebrity status."

Before a person becomes a Christian celebrity, he realizes that God is working *through* him. After he becomes a celebrity, he thinks he is working *for* God and that he's doing God's work. He may even delude himself into thinking his will is really God's will.

Those working to be celebrities are tempting God.

IS GOD USING ME OR AM I USING GOD?

I met Torrey Johnson when he first started Youth for Christ. At that time I was asking certain people I admired for their picture and autograph. He gave me his with the inscription: "To Fred, God's man in God's place." I never felt I could hang that on the wall. I kept it in the desk drawer. I was always condemned by how seldom I felt that I was truly God's man in God's place. During the times I felt God was using me, I felt extremely small and extremely secure. When I felt big, I felt insecure, because then I was depending on my own strength.

Recently when I asked a friend the usual question, "How's it going, Ron?" he answered in the best possible way. He said, "Fred, I feel God is using me." What a wonderful feeling to realize God is using us rather than our using God. So long as we keep that spiritual dimension in our leadership, people will see God in us.

Two great epitaphs come to mind: Someone told me he found the small gravestone of Fanny Crosby, which was located in the same cemetery as the large monument to Barnum, the circus king. Crosby's said simply, "Aunt Fanny—she did what she could."

The other great epitaph is the one for A. W. Tozer: "He was a man of God."

INNER SUCCESS

Once a young preacher said to me, "I can be happy just being a man of God, but that isn't enough for my family. It isn't enough for my board. They want me to be successful."

If we let others define our success, it is truly a slippery slope. If we follow Christ's example, then we simply go about doing good.

I suggest to any Christian who wants to be successful that he or she explore Scripture and try to find someone who started out to be successful and then made it. I can name five or six who tried it, and each was cursed. Remember the man who offered the apostles money for the spiritual gift? He probably intended to help people with it, but he wanted to take the credit instead of seeing that God got it. Peter told him, "May your money perish with you."

You may remember that Mother Teresa said she would not accept any more honors because it took time away from her work. Caring for the dying was more important than receiving the Nobel Prize. She knew inner success.

NARROWING THE GAP

A linguist with Wycliffe Bible Translators once told me that in twenty primitive languages the word for *belief* and *do* is the same. As we become more "sophisticated," we divide it into two words.

When our behavior contradicts our stated belief, it doesn't mean that we don't hold to the belief, but rather that it has become an intellectual position instead of a behavioral one. We can become so astute in the study of belief and the statement of belief that they become disconnected from behavior.

I've thought a great deal about the dichotomy of belief and behavior, and I find mine can result from a criminal arrogance. I say "criminal" because a common denominator of criminals is their belief that "the law doesn't apply to me." The dichotomy is also part of the spoiled-brat syndrome; I think I don't have to respect authority. Or I think like the politician—I *make* the laws, not obey them.

I can think the belief is right for everyone else but rationalize an exception for myself. This is not just sophistry, it is sin.

WHAT ARE YOU BECOMING?

Those around us will always judge us by our accomplishments. They will know what we have done, what we have built, where we have been, the jobs we've held, the titles we have worn, and the honors we have garnered. But on the inside, we continually ask ourselves, *Am I content with who I am becoming or who I have become?*

In east Texas we have the large pine beetle, which, when it dies, remains clinging to the bark of the pine tree. The insides dry up, and though the body of the insect appears to be alive, when you approach it, expecting it to fly away, you find it is but a hollow shell.

Occasionally I meet someone whose life has evaporated; he has become a walking hollow shell. His living has used up his life.

WHAT FEEDS THE SOUL?

I'm fond of reading the saints of old. (The original saints were, of course, Southern Baptists.) In their writings and meditations, I see nothing of planning to be successful or significant. They were not motivated by human ambition. The glory of God was their joy.

They were concerned not with God's plan for their life but his presence in their life. They seemed to feel that if they had a guide they didn't need a map. Both Brother Lawrence and Frank Laubach have written inspiringly on the presence of God.

Occasionally I speak to a Christian leader who seems hard and metallic. The more ambitious they are, the more metallic. Some with whom I have shared intimate moments seem dry on the inside. The soul can't be fed with ambition, accomplishment, and acquisition. The soul is fed by the Spirit and the words that proceed from God.

ACTIVITY OR ACCOMPLISHMENT?

I have learned that if I end my day feeling beat, I probably didn't accomplish much of anything worthwhile. Accomplishment gives me such a joy that it actually restores my energy. Activity for its own sake, on the other hand, is draining.

As I've gotten older, I've found the less I do the more I enjoy it because I'm more selective, more thorough, more conscious of what I'm trying to do. I've learned that activity is not the mark of accomplishment. The more I can delegate tasks that are not uniquely mine, the more attention I can pay to those that are.

A pastor may feel he doesn't have the luxury of doing a few things well, but the principles still apply. I have run small organizations, and I have run large organizations. I've never been short of time, because I believe I've been given an ability to prioritize what I'm trying to do. I retain to myself the things that only I can do and delegate the rest. It is easy to make the mistake of feeling important when people are depending on us.

I don't get joy from feeling needed. I have told my family that when I die, I hope they will not feel I was needed, but only loved. I want them each to mature to the point where they don't need me. To me, this is a proper leadership philosophy.

PHONY CONFESSIONS

Beware of self-serving confessions. Often confession can be used as advertising, such as the young man who confessed to buying expensive clothes. He didn't stop buying them, he just wanted them noticed. Another person in a small mixed group confessed to high sexual desire. Again, that was advertising, not confessing. He was dropping bits of honey hoping to find hungry flies.

The self-serving confession is often augmented according to audience reaction. I've heard Christian leaders use confession as a way of proving they are "one of the boys." The wisdom literature of Scripture tells us that "a fool exposes his folly." For a leader to say, "I'm a sinner, saved by grace" is different from laying out the proof of his sin.

Bishop Fulton Sheen conducted a retreat for priests and nuns. He stressed the point that if you are a priest, you must pay the price to be extraordinary; don't buy cheap comfort by confessing things you should keep to yourself. A leader should not be lured into the trap of exposing weaknesses as a way of saying, "Look how humble I am." Whenever we call attention to our humility, that is the ultimate in pride.

Overcoming Cynicism

Cynicism has no integrity. Cynicism often properly evaluates the present, but it has no hope for the future. As Christians we are not without hope for the future. Christians believe in the possibility of the future. Our responsibility is to make a difference, not to drop out.

Recently a bright, young executive asked me to lunch. He opened the conversation by saying, "I serve on several Christian boards and have been invited to join two national ministry boards. But as a businessman I have become cynical at what I see. You have been in it all your life. How have you avoided cynicism?"

I freely admitted that I have a certain amount of cynicism—I hope, healthy—I doubt that you can be in Christian service as long as I have without it. Nevertheless, I assured him that there is an antidote, which comes in two parts:

Maintain your sense of humor. I have found that any human activity, whether in religion or not, contains the frailties of the race. To me, healthy humor eases the tension between where we are and where we ought to be. Too often in the most serious business of the kingdom, we act as clowns in the court. We play games, indulge in politics, defend our errors, deny our temptations. All of these situations can be a great source for humor. Sins garbed in ecclesiastical raiment are ridiculous. In such situations, it's much better to laugh than to cry or criticize.

At the risk of being thought irreverent, I will tell you about an experience in which you wouldn't expect to find humor, but I did. It was at my father's funeral, held in a large church with many local ministers in attendance. Officiating were the new minister coming into the church and the older, longtime pastor who was leaving. They were both great showmen, and the situation was too overpowering for them not to try to outshine each other.

Shortly into the funeral, I wrote my brother a note: "Watch these two clowns outdo each other." One was known for his tremendous memory of Scripture. He reeled off reams of it. The other, older man was a great orator, and coming after the young preacher, he preached in high style, causing the angels to fly off the ramparts of heaven.

I wasn't offended, for I knew if my father could suddenly come alive, he would enjoy this as a delightful show; his Irish laugh would have been heard throughout the church. Both were men of fine spirit and sincerity who just got caught up in a situation that became a contest.

Look for the reality amid the counterfeit. The more counterfeit there is, the more I am convinced of the reality, for only reality promotes and protects counterfeit. Counterfeiters don't make $1 notes, they make $100 notes. Where I see counterfeit, I look for reality, for I know it's there.

FIGHT THE RIGHT FIGHT

When Paul said, "I have fought the good fight," he didn't mean with other Christians. Yes, the Christian life is a fight, but it isn't a fight against other believers. They are not the enemy. Satan is the Enemy. We lose integrity by fighting other members of the body. We are forbidden by Scripture to do this.

For years I was friends with a theologian who happily

accepted credit for starting a major conflict in his denomination. Once when he was castigating not only the views of the opposing leaders but also the leaders, I asked him, "Are they going to heaven?"

"Oh yes," he answered.

I asked, "Then what scriptural right do you have for kicking another member of the body? If they are going to heaven, they are a member of the body of Christ, and if I understand Scripture, it says we are not to pit one member of the body against the other."

A historian said that few battles over theology are ever caused by theology; they are power struggles, they are ego positions. They are strong leaders against strong leaders using theology as the basis for the fight, not the reason for it. Power, not theology, is at the heart of the struggle.

Well-meaning Christian leaders can be drawn into such battles because when dealing with bureaucracy, religious or corporate, the politically smart thing is to stay on the side of power. Therefore, we tend to identify ourselves with the interests of those in power. While I was in management, the union once had an organizing theme with the phrase "The banana that leaves the stalk gets peeled."

One Sunday I heard a brilliant young preacher take on a denominational fight that I had reason to believe he did not believe in. He was encouraged by an older pastor to jump into the fray. In the sermon, this young preacher smoked the opposition. I felt sad to see the animosity with which he used his great talent. Unfortunately, the man has now left the ministry and has had a rather disastrous life. I wonder whether part of it dates back to when, in order to gain favor, he took a position under duress.

The greatest defense we can give of the gospel is to personify it, not to argue it.

FROM FUNCTION TO FRIEND

Years ago I met John Stein, the famous impresario who brought several of the great stars to Broadway. When I asked him if there was a secret to the stars' popularity and longevity, he said, "They go on the platform as an entertainer; they come off as a person." He explained how they moved from function to friend. They were not interested in image; they were interested in the function and becoming real as individuals to the audience.

This is an important lesson in leadership. The great doctors I have known have been able to move from function to friend. Some remain scientists and others become friends. This applies, of course, to other fields of work as well. Anyone who has to maintain an image will suffer loneliness and alienation. The important thing is that there be a real person, a real friend, behind the competent function.

POLITICAL POSITIONING

To place an individual for political purposes in a position outside his gifting is leadership prostitution. God has endowed each person with a gift that can glorify God. When we use the person for political security for ourselves, regardless of that person's gift, we are using what should be for the glory of God to secure our political position.

I have listened to several Sunday school teachers who

had no gift for teaching. They were loyalists within the organization. Sometimes ministers are promoted to denominational administrative work, though they have no gift for the work. They hold the title while someone else does the work. Their function is loyalty to the ecclesiastical union.

Once I was asked to join a corporate executive committee by a friend, but when I told him I didn't think he was completely honest in his leadership, he agreed we should stay friends but that I should not be on his board. Political structuring based on loyalty to a leader and not to Christ lacks integrity.

A SUCCESSFUL CONDITION

Most of us view success as fame, accomplishment, and acquisition. Our society has chosen personality over character. Christian success must be built on character, not personality or skill. The great qualities in life are involved in the character of a person, such as wisdom, integrity, honesty, loyalty, faith, forgiveness, and love.

The Everyday Bible gives an interesting translation of Psalm 131: "Lord, my heart is not proud. I do not look down on others. I do not do great things and I cannot do miracles. But I am calm and quiet."

How can we claim Christian success unless our hearts are calm and quiet? Thomas Kelly, the eminent Quaker philosopher, said that inside each person there should be a quiet center that nothing can disturb. The great Catholic mystics continually talked of the throne of God, which is in the innermost part of our heart, where no storm, tribulation, or temptation can disturb.

Scripture says, "Greater is he that controls his spirit than he who takes a city." Obviously our condition is more than our accomplishment. In other words, our greatest accomplishment is our condition.

THE WISDOM PROCESS

There is a process to wisdom. First there are the bits of data that coagulate according to subjects into information. Then use is made of the information, which becomes knowledge. From knowledge we gain perspective of divine principles, which is wisdom. The greatest wisdom is revealed truth, not discovered truth.

Before knowledge can become wisdom, it has to pass through the mind and into the heart. With deep practicality, the Old Testament writings show the understanding of wisdom by referring to it as in the heart rather than in the mind—"out of the heart are the issues of life." Wisdom can be taught as principles, but it cannot become personal until it is practiced.

Wisdom is truth, and truth is eternal, and eternal is current. Therefore, there is no updating or out-of-dating of truth.

PART II

DEVELOPING YOUR SKILLS

6
IDENTIFYING THE MANDATE

MAX De PREE, FORMER CEO AND AUTHOR of *Leadership Jazz*, once said, "The number one responsibility of top management is to define reality."

That's true whether we're leading a corporation or a church, and establishing a mandate helps us to define that reality and to lead with integrity. Leaders need to ask, "Why are we operating? What are we about? What are we dedicated to?" Once these questions have been addressed and a consensus around their answers developed, a leader has a mandate, a foundation out of which to determine programs, recruit leadership, establish organizational culture, and figure out what and what not to do.

One critical function of a mandate is that it separates loyalty to the leader from loyalty to the cause. The leader has to say, "I am subservient to this mandate. You don't serve me. You don't make me happy. And don't keep me in charge unless I fulfill the mandate."

I was talking to ten pastors who all have Ph.D. degrees.

One asked, "How can I get my church to do my program?"

I responded by asking him two questions. The first was, "Did you found the church?" No, he didn't. The second was, "Would you leave if you got a better offer?" Yes, he would leave.

"Then what right do you have to call it 'my' church?" I replied. "You'd be better off saying 'our' church."

While the leader is responsible for the initiation of the mandate, he has to build a consensus for it among people—first, that they buy into the mandate, and second, that they are willing to dedicate themselves to carrying it out.

Often leaders will put their friends, their associates, their politically loyal people into key positions, whether or not they belong there. It's easy to fall into this double agenda, this popularity contest. But we're not in leadership to become popular; we're there to advance the mandate.

The other danger with an organization centered on a leader rather than a mission is that when the leader leaves, his people may follow and leave no effective group vested in the cause and dedicated to carrying on the mission.

Narrowing the focus

You have to be careful, however, not to set out what I call a "Mother Hubbard mandate"—there needs to be specificity in the mandate. Too many churches and organizations get trapped in a mission statement that sounds good but is too general to be effective. The mission statement is empty of meaning. For example, a church might have as its mission statement, "For the glory of God and the good of man." Ultimately, any church is called to work toward that end, but that can be interpreted in many different ways. Such a statement does not set out a workable basis for ministry.

Some churches try to put their mandate in their name—"Bible Church," "Fellowship Church," "Church of Christ." Yet these names and ideas are not specific enough for leaders to lead effectively. The focus of the mandate must be specific and clear so that everyone knows exactly what is meant by it. In fact, it should not be possible to interpret a mandate except in a narrow sense. That discipline enables the leader to set boundaries. A leader defines the organizational culture and develops programs within the established boundaries set by the mandate.

No church can accomplish everything. I once heard a pastor say, "I can't make a mark on infinity. My mark has to be on finiteness." Maybe huge organizations can accomplish a great array of things, but the average church has to identify its strengths and choose where it will put its efforts.

The big three

Within the life of any church, there are three broad umbrella areas—what the church is about—out of which a mandate must be drawn.

First, the church is about the salvation of the lost. Second, it's about the maturing of the saved. And third, it's about the spiritual fellowship of the saints—the believers. All evaluations of a church's mission and activities need to proceed from these three fundamentals.

Let's say, for example, that a church decides its mandate is evangelism. Then going out and reaching the unsaved is what they are about. They have to ask themselves, "What are we going to do to win the lost? What is our specific program? How best can we appeal to the nonbeliever?"

According to church consultant Lyle Schaller, as much as 85 percent of "church growth" is actually transfer growth. If the church whose mandate is to reach the lost is in reality only attracting other Christians, then that church is merely poaching other churches. It isn't evangelizing. Such churches have to come back to their mandate.

It's the same with maturing the saved. First, a church has to define a "mature Christian." Then it has to determine what activities will accomplish this end. A leader must to be able to give honest answers to these questions: Are people more mature today than they were last year? How have they grown? What sermon series were done? What Sunday school programs? What are the evidences of maturity?

Regarding spiritual fellowship, the same kind of honesty and objectivity applies. I see a lot of activities in the church, but many are not always for spiritual fellowship; they're for social fellowship. Even Bible studies and small groups may not bring about that kind of spiritual growth and connecting. Are people learning accountability? Is there a sense of strength, of belonging? Are Christians striving for Christlikeness?

It's important to distinguish a program from a mandate. Programs come and go, and they should. Leaders should always be looking at programs in light of whether they serve the mandate. If they don't, they should be cut.

Evaluation tool

I remember the words of a German bandmaster at our children's school. He had a championship band, and whenever he disciplined anybody, he always said, "You can't play like that and play in this band." He never said, "You can't play like that and play for me." He didn't equate personal loyalty with a person's contribution to the cause. He believed that unless you were willing to contribute everything you had, you didn't belong.

When a leader is sure of the mandate, he or she can create a more effective leadership team. One can discipline and evaluate people in light of the mandate. I've been reading an excellent book about leadership as exemplified by four-star generals and admirals. It's clear these leaders knew exactly what the military was trying to do, and their selection of people was based entirely on their ability to contribute to what they were charged with doing. Selection is largely determined by the mandate.

So is the development of people. When a leader finds someone who has potential to fulfill the mandate but needs developing, then that leader should know exactly how to bring him or her along. Likewise, if someone is not moving the mandate forward by his or her activity, then that activity should be stopped.

I used to say I was certain my friend Maxey Jarman, chairman of Genesco and also my superior at work, would have asked me to leave any time he felt I was hurting the organization. Then he would have taken me to lunch. It was his responsibility to see that everybody in the organization, friend and foe, was contributing to the organization's welfare.

Even if he'd taken my job, I still would have gone to lunch with him as a dear friend. I would have respected his judgment that I was not advancing the mandate.

A mandate gives a leader the ability to define the leadership he needs. Once I asked a pastor of a fast-growing church, "What is your emphasis?"

Upward mobility, he responded. "You show me another church with eight thousand members, where the chairman of the board is thirty-two years old," he said. "Young people are not willing to wait for promotions in business, and I don't think they ought to have to wait in church."

Part of his mandate, then, was the utilization of up-and-coming young leaders. His mandate was helping him define his leadership.

Call or mandate?

There's a difference between a mandate and a call. A call is personal; it comes to the individual. A mandate is collective, corporate. The mandate is the organization's reason for being; the call is the individual's reason for service.

A leader needs to have a sense of call, of dedication, to serve effectively. Prison evangelist Bill Glass emphasizes this in training his prison counselors. He says, "You have volunteered to be a counselor, but you have dedicated your life to personify Christ in this prison." He goes through a litany of experiences that a volunteer might not be able to take (e.g., getting cussed out, having urine thrown on him). But the dedicated counselor will hang in.

A call may change. A person might sense a call to a different organization or a different form of service. Sometimes I think the call may lead someone out of the ministry.

Recently I talked with a pastor in Iowa whose primary ministry was teaching the Bible. I asked him how he was doing, and he admitted he was unhappy. So were the people. I asked him, "What is your real love?"

"My real love is winning people to Christ," he said.

"In your saint-saturated organization," I said, "there is nobody to win. And whenever you get up to teach, you don't see a single soul who needs salvation, and yet you are by nature an evangelist. Have you considered leaving the ministry and going back into automobile sales, where you're constantly in contact with lost people?"

"That's when I was happiest," he said.

But he had let his ego get involved, and he became a pastor. Now he has moved back into sales and is extremely happy and effective. His call—to win people—did not match the organization he was serving. I know several people who would be much happier if they would recognize they haven't been called to what they're doing.

The simplest form

As leaders think about the mandate for their particular organization, they should remember that the simplest way it can be accomplished is the most effective. Organizations tend to let what they do become too complicated.

The head of an international ministry came to me with several sheets of paper, laying out an organizational chart. After I had reviewed it, I said, "Evidently somebody in your organization is studying management material. I'm all for that, except there are only two questions you need to answer starting out: Number one, what are you really trying to do? Number two, what is the simplest way you can do it?"

As we talked, he said, "It's very simple for me to know what we're trying to do."

"Then forget the drawing," I said. "It's not the simplest way you can do it. It is a complicated system that involves a lot of people's ambitions, ego, and comfort. The ambitions and ego need to be weeded out."

He went back to his board with a new statement, and they were grateful somebody had come up with a simpler way to carry out the work of the organization.

If I were drawing up a new mandate for an organization in trouble, I would figure out the simplest way of accomplishing what it set out to do. Not that this is always simple to do; I'm trying to find the simplest way a task can be done. Albert Einstein once said that whatever God does, he does in its simplest form. And how can we improve upon that?

7

DISCERNING THE PEOPLE YOU LEAD

IF THE LORD HAS BLESSED YOU with the gift of discernment, use it in your leadership. Our gifts are our uniqueness, and our greatest spiritual strength is always in the uniqueness of who we are. You reach integrity by being who you are in all the fullness God intended. The false self is the person whom you try to imitate. The most grateful compliment we can pay our Creator is to fulfill and optimize our uniqueness. How can we pray, asking God to make us someone we aren't or to do something we are not gifted to do? Our leading should be according to who we are.

I have known many excellent leaders who were not given the gift of discernment. They could not read people. They could read figures. They excelled in science, engineering, mathematics, and administration. They depended on management skills, behavioral research, organizational charts, methods, and the types of learned skills taught in business school.

Those blessed with discernment, however, develop sensitivity, empathy, and intuition. I am one of these types, having used discernment for many years both in manufacturing (twenty-five hundred employees) and in ministry (chairman of several national ministries).

I was fortunate in my career to have both Ray Stedman, pastor of Peninsula Bible Church, and Baxter Ball, vice-president of Mobil, verify my discernment and intuition. They encouraged me to use these in my leadership. Early on, my mentor Maxey Jarman emphasized utilizing strength and buttressing weakness. I had natural leadership gifts and a strong desire to lead but little training in the usual skills.

A word about my background may be helpful to you: My father was pastor of a small blue-collar church. I never heard the word *business* mentioned in my home. After graduating from high school, I went out to find a job, my first experience in business. At age twenty-six I became head of a corporate function and by my early thirties a vice-president of operations. I was weak with numbers, and disliked the monotony of administration. In addition, I was not blessed with great physical energy. I never had the urge to rush from one thing to another, keeping a lot of balls in the air. I'm not a type-A personality.

I realized that both numbers and administration were vital. I overcame my lack in the numbers area by always having a capable numbers person with me. I picked an assistant who enjoyed detail to follow up on routine administration.

My strength was in vision, picking and placing people, and coordinating their efforts. Here my discernment was a tremendous help to me.

I was encouraged to use and develop discernment skills by a simple statement of the revered retailer John Wanamaker, who said, "A mule balks in his head before he balks in his feet, and so do people." Another confirmation came in reading a survey made of the New York Philharmonic Orchestra about who had been the most effective director. Toscanini won it, hands down. When asked about his strength, one of the players said, "He could anticipate when you were about to make a mistake and keep you from making it."

He had discernment.

Later I found another confirming illustration. The manufacturing company for which I was vice-president of operations made high-precision instruments. For years the quality control was put on the individual piece as it went through operation after operation. When an operation damaged the piece in the process, it was very expensive. Our engineers developed a method of establishing the control on the machine as well as on the part. When a machine was going out of tolerance, they would shut it down before it damaged parts.

While individuals obviously vary much more than machines, I found that if I could read people correctly, I could keep up their productivity and minimize their mistakes.

Discernment, like musical talent, is innate; however, both must be practiced and developed. Simply having the gift of music does not make one a concert pianist.

Learning to listen and observe

Words are the windows to the mind. Socrates said, "Speak, young man, that I might know you." Productive listening is active and intense listening. It is hearing more than words. Most of the time we grasp just enough of what

generally well understood. Often what it becomes is simply older men visiting with younger men without an agenda. These visits sometimes turn into Bible study or prayer times. These are excellent activities, but they are not mentoring.

Mentoring is a one-on-one relation between a mentor and mentoree for the specific and definable development of a skill or an art. One of my favorite mentoring stories is of the young pianist who came to Leonard Bernstein and asked to be mentored by him. Bernstein said, "Tell me what you want to do, and I will tell you whether or not you're doing it." When you analyze this, you realize Bernstein's deep understanding of mentoring. The young man initiated the contact, he had a specific request, and he made the request of an authority—not that he might get rich as a concert pianist or famous like Bernstein, but that he might become a better pianist.

Bernstein essentially said to the young man, "You're responsible for your playing and your practice. The one thing you can't do is hear yourself as a great pianist hears you. That I can do and will do for you."

The study of mentoring can be organized, but not the application of it. Effective mentoring has no set formula. It's a living relationship and progresses in fits and starts. It can involve a specific area or several areas. For example, one big area of need is the improvement of decision-making. Goal-setting is another. However, these must be specific. The goal may be broad, but in skills-art mentoring it must be specific.

I've discovered it is not difficult to make a list of desired characteristics in a mentor. However, like characteristics of a leader, they are in combination and not equally balanced. To some degree, however, each of these qualities should be in a mentor:

1. *The two must share a compatible philosophy.* Our goals and methods are really an expression of our philosophy. If the goal is to be Christian, the philosophy must be built on divine principles. To me, wisdom is the knowledge and application of scriptural principles; not the citing of verses or telling of stories, but the definition of the principles. I usually illustrate this by the biblical principle: "God will not do for you what you can do for yourself, nor will he let you do for yourself what only he can do."

It is wrong to pray for a miracle, for instance, when God has given us the mental ability, opportunity, and facilities to accomplish what we should do. To ask for a miracle is to ask God to be redundant. But he will not let us do for ourselves what only he can do. For example, he will not let us gain our salvation by works; it is only by his grace.

On the other hand, if the goal is based on humanistic values, then the result will be cultural, not Christian. Human philosophy often exploits our greed and selfishness. Human philosophy promotes self-love and self-aggrandizement. Recently a young man came to me asking that I help him "make a million dollars." That was his life's goal. He has a materialistic, humanistic philosophy.

I told him that we did not agree on philosophy; therefore, I would not be a good mentor for him.

2. *The mentor should be knowledgeable in the subject and objective in his criticism.* The mentor who simply says what the other wants to hear is irresponsible. He should not counsel in matters in which he is not an expert or pass judgment

in subjects beyond his limitation. The young pianist was right in going to Bernstein, because he was an authority, a knowledgeable expert, and an objective critic for the young pianist.

It is important that the mentor on occasion admit, "I don't know. I've had no experience with that." It is good when he has a broad network of knowledgeable friends who might be helpful on occasion. That is one of the strengths of Mayo Clinic. It can call in experts when an individual doctor gets beyond his or her expertise.

Once a young, brash president of a growing corporation was being dangerously extravagant. Though I was on the board, he wasn't accepting my authority on the subject. I got him an appointment with the CEO of a major corporation, who successfully warned him and possibly saved the company.

3. *The mentor must genuinely believe in the potential of the mentoree.* A mentor cannot do serious thinking about the needs of the learner or spend the necessary time with him without believing in his potential. A mentor isn't doing what he's doing to be a nice guy. Then there may be times when the learner loses confidence in himself, particularly after a failure, and he will need the mentor to restore his confidence.

I had breakfast with a young executive in Dallas, and I asked him to tell me his story. He said, "Until early in my twenties, I amounted to nothing. I think that was due to the fact that I was raised in a fundamentalist family who believed it was wrong to say anything good about anyone that might stir up his pride. I felt there was nothing special about me until my Sunday school teacher put his arm around my shoulders and said, 'I believe in you.' "

Gradually this young man began to believe in himself. From that time, he started to climb the executive ladder.

4. *A good mentor helps define the vision, the goal, and the plan.* So many young men I talk to have several options for their life, and they are not equipped to choose the right one. They hesitate at the thought of giving up the others.

Recently I had lunch with a young man who graduated from a prestigious European university with high marks and told me he had "tested genius in thirteen areas." Yet he had done nothing, though he was in his early thirties. I was talking to another man in the same general circumstances, and I said, "You could have married six or eight girls, but you chose one. You will have to do the same with your goal."

Choosing a specific goal is the key to many other activities. The goal defines the discipline, creates the energy, and gives the measure of progress.

Clarifying the goal is a crucial step in the mentoring process. It controls so many other elements. I try to find whether the individual's goal is formed by outside or inside influences. Is his accomplishment to please or impress others or to satisfy himself? The image of success has become prevalent in our society. I want to know what gives him his deepest satisfaction. What, to him, has meaning? What does he do easily? What does he learn quickly and remember clearly? Is the goal realistic, considering his talent, opportunities, and facilities?

Sometimes a person will say, "I know where I want to go, but I don't know how to get there." I have found it much easier to work out the map once you know the destination. Be sure the plan is as simple as it can be. Elaborate plans seldom get carried out. Too often, complicated plans are a subconscious attempt to avoid doing.

Paul J. Meyer, creator of Sales Motivation Institute, spent the day with me when he was a young salesman going over the four-step program he had for his life. I was so impressed I asked him for a copy, and he gave me the original, written on a piece of yellow paper, which I still have in my files. In our original conversation, he said that after you set the specific goal, you work the plan, then forget the goal, and develop enthusiasm for the plan, knowing that if you work the plan, you will reach the goal.

5. *The chemistry must be good.* The first evidence of this is clear communication. Each must clearly and easily understand the other. Before I start to work with someone, I check this out by talking for a few minutes and then asking the person to repeat what I've said. Sometimes I'm amazed at what I hear. It's difficult to work well together unless each communicates well with the other.

Intuition—a feeling of the spirit of each other—is also important. When our spirits are in harmony, then we can work until our communications are clear. We won't jump to conclusions or get carried off into prejudices. I find this particularly true when working between races.

Often our communications are controlled by certain grids. For example, our value system is a grid. If someone said to me, "I don't believe the Bible," that would immediately get stopped by my value grid. I would find myself subconsciously devaluing what that person said. There are several grids through which our communications must go.

Communication, to me, is understanding, not

agreement. I hear people say that their problem is a lack of communication, when it may actually be genuine difference of opinion. No amount of communication will change that.

6. *The mentor needs the experience and originality to develop options rather than decisions.* Often individuals with whom I work initially become frustrated that I will not give them advice but rather options from which they can choose. If I give advice, then I'm taking over responsibility for their decision-making, and that is not my function. Furthermore, how a decision is carried out is as important as the decision, and the mentor can't control the carrying out.

The mentor must never take over the decision-making responsibility for the individual. After the mentor has given options and ramifications, an intelligent learner will generally select the correct one, the one he believes in most and therefore the one that will get his best effort. A good mentor is not a quick-fix artist.

7. *The mentor must be able to commit to a person and to a situation.* Once I was involved in a land development requiring large amounts of money from a New England bank. The loan officer was careful in exploring all the details. He explained, "Don't think I'm being too careful. I don't want to get you halfway across the river." When we commit to a mentor, we commit to the person all the way across. That will take time and thinking. I must be willing to take a phone call any time it comes from a mentoree in stress.

8. *The mentor must be given the responsibility to hold the mentoree accountable.* That the mentoree gives this responsibility to the mentor is important, because this avoids his

becoming resentful or quietly rebellious or hostile. Accountability is a major feature of mentoring.

I tell one of my mentorees that my accountability factor is like the tail on a kite—it keeps it from darting around. Accountability is not control. In mentoring it is pointing out objectively what is happening and asking if that is what the mentoree wants. At no time should the mentor take control over the other's life. The mentor is a counselor, not a boss.

Accountability is confined to the area of mentoring. It is not open season on all areas of a person's life. If we are mentoring in professional matters, it doesn't give us the right to invade family matters.

Traits of a good mentoree

There are also certain traits essential to an effective mentoree. Some may have to be developed more as the relationship develops.

1. *The mentoree must be honest with himself.* Effective mentoring must be based on reality. To me, two of the most important words in life are "current reality." That means being committed to things as they are, not as we wish they were. We may want them to be different and be willing to work to make them different, but for the present we have to deal with things as they are. I am particularly sensitive to what the psychologists call "transference." The mentoree must own the situation before he can correct it or develop it.

Recently I stopped working with a young man because he had been dishonest about his financial situation. He admitted he was in debt but said that it was his wife's fault, which he couldn't control. A prominent psychiatrist once told me that America's second greatest sin, after refusing to delay gratification, is transference, at the heart of so much of the victim syndrome. Those who feel they are victims generally expect more than they are due.

I applaud the individual who is handicapped in some way (mentally, socially, physically) but has accepted it as a challenge and no longer sees himself as a victim but as a victor. It's easy to work a little harder and a little longer with people who think that way. An executive I've admired for years had an eye put out when he was a small boy. When he entered an Ivy League school, he checked the records and found that no one had ever made straight As and four letters in athletics. He did it, with one eye. He later became vice-president of a major corporation. He was a winner, not a victim.

2. *A mentoree must be a good student.* A truly good student enjoys the growth process as well as the reward. When I became intrigued with golf, I thoroughly enjoyed the practice and the study of the game. Great teachers want to find great students. With my mentor I tried to be a good student. That entailed several things for me:

First, I never tried to impress him with my knowledge. I always exposed to him my ignorance. To hide my ignorance from a teacher is as foolish as hiding my sickness from a doctor. A humble person is always conscious of his ignorance more than his knowledge.

Dr. Walter Hearn, who was a biochemist at Yale University, surprised me once by saying, "Fred, every night when you go to bed you ought to be more ignorant than you were when you woke up." I took this facetiously until he explained that if I thought of my knowledge as a balloon and every day that balloon increased in size, it would touch more and more ignorance on the periphery. Therefore my knowledge brought me into contact with my greater ignorance. The arrogant are proud of their knowledge; the humble are acquainted with their ignorance.

A good student never tries to "use" his mentor. A person with a well-known mentor can be tempted to refer to him in ways that really use him, particularly in quoting him out of context. The mentor is for progress, not ego satisfaction. On a few occasions I have been abused by someone claiming me as his mentor when there was no relation.

A good student works to ask the right questions. Right questions come from thought, analysis, and discernment. He never asks an idle or careless question. It is demeaning to the mentor. There is power in a good question. Recently a young professor told me how following an awards program he asked a prominent man two questions, and the man concentrated on answering only those two questions to the disregard of all those trying to shake hands with him. I have found writing out my questions beforehand helpful in minimizing the verbiage.

A good student does his homework. In dealing with my two mentors, I never called them unless I had written down on paper what I wanted to talk to them about. When we met, I had organized my questions; I knew it was not a social situation. If later we wanted to spend some social time together, that would be up to them, not me.

In fact, I never walked into their office and sat down

until I was invited to sit down. They had to know I was not going to waste their time.

3. *The mentoree must show reasonable progress.* Progress is the pay the mentoree gives the mentor. Currently I spend at least 50 percent of my time mentoring talented individuals. I make no charge. But I get amply paid by the vicarious accomplishments of these individuals. Putting our lives into the lives of others is the best way to attain human immortality.

In the New York obituary of my mentor, it said, "The awesome intellect of him is gone." I can refute that, for as long as I and others whom he mentored live, he lives.

4. *The mentoree needs to develop disciplines to maintain his gains.* Discipline always starts with a habit, and when the habit is practiced enough it turns into a reflex, and then it doesn't have to be consciously done anymore.

Our disciplines should be more positive than negative. The only reason we employ negative disciplines is to help us perform the positive ones. Unfortunately, in Christian circles a lot of people practice negative disciplines and consider this Christianity. They don't realize the negatives are practiced in order to release time, energy, and resources to do the positive.

Let me show you what I mean with a silly illustration: Your wife sends your son to the grocery store for a loaf of bread. She gives him the money, asks him to hurry, not to stop and play with his friends, not to get dirty, and not to lose the money. He hurries off and comes back without the bread. When she questions him, he says, "You told me to hurry. I did. You told me not to stop to play. I didn't. You said not to get dirty. I didn't. You said not to lose the money, and I didn't. I didn't do what you told me not to do."

Nor did he get the bread. The negatives were to promote him in the positive of getting the bread. He avoided the negatives but didn't complete the positive. Too often we police people with the negatives rather than inspire them with the positives.

5. *The mentoree must possess vision and commitment.* As a mentoree, the two most important elements are vision and commitment. A clear vision and unconditional commitment are absolutely necessary. History is replete with illustrations of great accomplishments by ordinary individuals with extraordinary vision and commitment.

I vaguely recall a story about an ancient philosopher who when asked by a young man how he could get wisdom, took the young man down to the stream and held his head under the water until he nearly drowned. When he let the young man up, the philosopher said, "Long for wisdom like you longed for air, and you will get it."

There must be desire and passion for accomplishment—definable accomplishment.

I do not know how to instill passion in a mentoree. As a mentor, I try to channel it. I have found that continually reviewing the vision renews the passion. The passion works the plan, overcoming disappointments, and the plan accomplishes the goal.

Ten principles of a fruitful relationship

To close this chapter, let me mention several additional mentoring principles:

First, in a healthy mentoring relationship, all the cards are on the table. That involves trust between the two. I am careful not to tell my wife confidential matters that are told to me. Anything given in confidence should be held in confidence.

Second, though I have been mentoring actively for more than forty years, I cannot claim any success in improving character in adults. I have become convinced that the only improvement in character in adults is through spiritual experience, not through mentoring. Sophisticated individuals may learn to mask or hide their character flaws, but under excessive pressure they will fail. Character failures come at the most crucial time, when they can least be afforded. Dishonesty, laziness, anger, greed, selfishness, uncooperativeness—all are character failures.

Third, we progress by climbing, then plateauing for assimilation, then climbing again, plateauing again—repeating the process as long as we live. Unfortunately, many people reach a comfortable plateau and stop. They become seduced by comfort and routine. It is the mentor's challenge to see in the mentoree a potential he does not see and to motivate him to make another climb and another plateau, and then another and another, until his full talent is developed.

Fourth, not everyone can be a mentor, just as many superior performers cannot coach. Skill in performing and skill in coaching are very different. Most successful leaders have had good mentors, just as successful athletes have had good coaches.

Fifth, every good man should be good at something. Helping to develop this good is the mentor's responsibility.

Management expert Peter Drucker has the correct idea of mentoring. When someone says of another, "He is a good man," Peter asks, "Good for what?"

Sixth, a mentor has accomplished great good when he has taught the individual the joy of accomplishment. I learned this from my mentor, Maxey Jarman. It has become so much a part of my life that when I get low, I immediately start to do something that I feel will be worthwhile. The joy of living returns.

The great opera diva Beverly Sills personified this philosophy when one afternoon at a cocktail party in her apartment one guest said, "We'd better leave, Beverly has to sing tonight." She protested, "No, I don't have to sing tonight. I *get* to sing tonight."

Seventh, as we progress in our relationship we should come to the place where we need no preface or qualification. My two great mentors never prefaced with me. At first that seemed rather discourteous, and then I realized they were paying me the ultimate compliment of saying that I wanted to know truth and they didn't have to adjust it or varnish it.

Eighth, the mentor has a responsibility to create an atmosphere in which the learner can be honest and still respected. In good communication we need to avoid two disruptions: Never show shock at anything anyone says, for in showing shock we are setting our value structure against theirs. Instead of verbalizing shock, I like to say something neutral or noncommittal. If appropriate, I will even try to say something humorous to prevent ill feelings.

Never show curiosity. Curiosity hurts good communication. I think we all would like for people to be interested in us but not curious about us. Curiosity is an invasion of our privacy and generally comes out of a question that has nothing to do with the main purpose of the communication. For example, if someone told me he was having an affair, I would never ask with whom. If he wants to tell me, that is his call.

Ninth, I make the mentoree responsible for all contact. The individual must set up the appointment, make the calls, and so forth. I do this for a reason: I want the mentoree to know that he can break off the relationship any time he wants to simply by not contacting me. He controls the continuation of the relationship. I will never question why. Sometimes a mentoring relationship becomes nonproductive and should end. I accept this as normal.

Tenth, mutual respect is crucial. I have never had any success helping anyone I did not respect. I've tried but failed miserably.

Joy of mentoring

My favorite title is "mentor." Zig Ziglar flattered me, after years of publicly referring to me as his mentor, by dedicating *Over the Top* to me. I shouldn't repeat it, but since I'm over the hill rather than over the top, here is what he wrote:

"To my friend and mentor Fred Smith, Sr., who is fun and inspiring. He is also the wisest and most effective teacher I've ever had."

I hope you sense the seriousness and joy I feel in mentoring.

11

ESSAYS ON COMPETENCE

MAINTAIN THE VALUE OF COMPLIMENTS

Compliments are so valuable they should be used sparingly in order to remain valuable. Nothing was more disturbing to me than to be paired in a round of golf with an overly courteous individual who complimented my every shot—good, bad, and mediocre. He insulted my intelligence, as if I didn't know when I had made a good or bad shot.

Charles Pitts was an excellent golfer who complimented only "a golf shot." I can remember well on the ninth hole when I hit a ball with an eight iron—high over a tree—that landed reasonably close to the pin. He walked across the fairway, shook hands with me, and said, "That's a golf shot." He knew how to keep his compliments valuable.

If we overcompliment, we not only become a Pollyanna, we lose our authority to praise. Praise should be earned. It should be specific and come from someone who knows what he's complimenting. General Maxwell Taylor said

153

that you can cheapen yourself if you are too quick to give compliments. Compliments remain valuable when they have integrity and are given at the right time for the right reason.

THE CARE OF COCKLEBURS

Someone said every dog needed a flea to remind him that he is a dog. Most organizations need what my mentor Maxey Jarman called "corporate cockleburs."

Genesco had one of the best in Lou Sutley. Mr. Jarman put him on many of the operating committees just for his dissenting value. He was highly intelligent and saw the other side of most questions, which Maxey felt should be looked at even though doing so was unpleasant. Once I was chairing a meeting in which Lou punctured several sacred balloons. I became so frustrated that I went to see Mr. Jarman in a huff and threatened not to sit in another meeting with Lou. Mr. Jarman smiled and said, "He evidently is doing his job well. He's the corporate cocklebur. We need him." Valuable cockleburs are scarce and should be carefully cultivated.

Intelligent opposition dedicated to the cause may by disagreeing with us energize an integrity and courage that we can use to accomplish the mandate for our organization.

FAITH OR FOLLY?

There is a marked difference between scriptural faith and foolish assumptions. Wise faith responds to the promises and principles of Scripture. Folly faith is fueled by human desire, generally rationalized by deceptive proof-texting.

A few years ago, I was teaching a Presbyterian Sunday school class on David. I pointed out that he carried the five stones because as a good entrepreneur he didn't want to be undercapitalized. I opined that he knew if he missed Goliath with the first one, he certainly had a better than even chance of getting him with one out of the five, considering his skill. A dear lady confronted me after the class saying, "That can't be right. You never fail when you're working for God."

"What about Stephen?" I asked. All the martyrs were working for God.

When we abuse prayer, we are practicing faith folly. Too often prayer does not enter into the setting of our goals nearly as much as it does in the attaining of them. Better to seek God's will in the setting than to ask him to bless the accomplishment. We should pour prayer over our human efforts like sauce over meat.

WHO SETS OUR PRIORITY?

Years ago, Dick Halverson, former Senate chaplain, and I conducted a retreat for laypeople. He gave me great freedom when he said, "Do you realize that Christ did not have a daily planner? He simply went about doing good. When the woman with the sickness stopped him as he was going to raise the dead, he simply took care of it. He didn't say, 'Wait a minute. I'm on my way to raise the dead and that's more important than stopping your issue of blood.' He simply used each opportunity to do good. When we believe that God engineers our circumstances, he sets our priority."

As I get older I have come to a better perspective on how God engineers our circumstances. When I was young, I was a great planner. I still believe in planning organizational activities. However, I've learned to leave a flexibility in my spiritual service. Now I see instances that seemed insignificant at the time that were actually tremendously significant. A conversation with someone at the time might mean little yet might change a life.

I had breakfast with a young professional and gave him one thought, which he wrote down. Later he told me, "That re-vectored my life."

USE AND ABUSE OF HUMOR

For years I've studied the serious use of humor. I once asked Malcolm Muggeridge if there had ever been a book written about it and he said yes—there were two, and both were dreary because the men writing failed to have a sense of humor. Most books about humor end up as joke books and not about the use of humor.

We all recognize humor as a relief from hostility and rising tempers. Humor can be the softest of soft answers. Humor can be a coagulating agent for diverse groups in an audience. It is often used to give a psychological break when sustained thinking becomes tired.

There are many misuses of humor. I'll mention only three. First is the person who tells a story as if it happened to him. Since most people in the audience have likely heard the story many times before from many different people, such a tack not only decreases the effect of the story but impinges on the integrity of the teller.

Second, using too much humor causes listeners to wait for the next laugh and thus ignore the serious part of the talk. Laughs generally are much more appreciated than thoughts by the average person. That is evidenced in our society being saturated with entertainment.

Third, our humor should be theologically correct. I doubt we should ever laugh about hell or immorality. I've seen cartoons in Christian publications that were contrary to their stated theological beliefs.

Humor should illustrate a basic principle more than it should be decorative. The more we see good humor in human situations, the more they serve as excellent illustrations. Another important use of humor is to lubricate the needle. Some are so gifted in the use of humor that several minutes after we are away from them, we realize we were inoculated by truth with a needle lubricated with healthy humor.

CONSISTENCY IS VITAL

Followers basically want to align with their leader, but they must have a clear idea of how to do it. The leader's consistency is the answer.

An inconsistent leader confuses his followers. This creates a vacuum of leadership in which the aggressive go off on their own while the majority become immobilized, not knowing what to do for fear of making a mistake. A psychiatrist told me, "Be sure your employees know what makes you smile and what makes you frown. Be consistent. Always smile at the same thing and frown at the same thing, so your people know how to make you smile and how to avoid your frown. Employees feel secure when they know they are helping the boss to smile."

THE FALSE TEST OF SPIRITUAL ENDEAVORS

Recently I attended a *Guideposts* seminar on "The Power of Positive Thinking in Business." One attendee was a bright executive, vice-president of a large corporation. During the break she wanted to visit with me, because she'd heard of my having mentored executives.

In our conversation, she mentioned, "I used to be a Methodist, but now I'm all-out New Age, and *it works for me.*" She said it with such emphasis, conviction, and triumph that I wanted to learn more of her story, but the break ended. Often I have heard leaders claim God's blessings on their efforts because "it works." Many times we rationalize a questionable method as practical because "it works."

But is "working" the real test of spiritual endeavors?

A friend, Warren Hultgren, once pointed out to me that "working" isn't the perfect test, for Moses struck the rock twice and it worked. That is, water came out—but he was kept from the Promised Land. Our nonscriptural human methods might work, but do they keep us from entering the "Promised Land" of peace and joy?

SINCERITY IN COMMUNICATION

When we want to communicate, we must accept our responsibility to use language the other understands. Nonbelievers, particularly those without a Christian background in church or family, hear many of our revered standard phrases as pious babble. Even our tone of voice turns them off. We have adopted the seminary brogue so widely that when surfing the TV, we can tell a sermon by only a word or two.

Using "blessed hope" and "saved" means a lot to those who have it and are, but nothing to those outside the Christian community. We must have enough passion to communicate that we learn the language of those outside our ranks and then use it meaningfully. In Mexico, I find myself frustrated by the inability of its people to understand English rather than by my inability to speak Spanish. Comically, I find myself talking louder and repeating myself more as if repetition and volume could create understanding.

Within the Christian community, sincerity of communication must be a hallmark; we must be careful not to use our assumed personal connection with God as a persuasion tool.

HEALTHY ATTRITION

A certain attrition rate in aspiring leadership is healthy. The Army has 7 percent, the Marines 14, and some of the drill sergeants think it should be as high as 25. "Beware of him of whom all men speak well" should apply to our leadership—not that we go out to disqualify people, but we should not maintain people who disqualify themselves, either by lack of character or gifts.

I started out as a voice student hoping to make the

opera. Fortunately, I had an honest teacher who one morning after a lesson said, "Fred, you have everything to be a successful singer except talent. You can't make it. Don't waste your life trying." He was so right and so courageous. He blessed me with his honesty. I went into business where I had a talent. Remember what Spurgeon told his young students: "Young man, if you can't speak, you weren't called to preach."

BREAKING PSYCHOLOGICAL BARRIERS

Roger Bannister did more than run the first four-minute mile in history. He broke a psychological barrier. Almost immediately, others started doing what had never been done before. They, too, ran the mile in under four minutes. Training couldn't account for that; there wasn't that much time between when he broke the record and when others also began running under four minutes.

Leaders need to recognize and break psychological barriers for their people. The greatest barrier I have seen in the church is: "The deeper life is not for me. Only a few are caught in the web of his grace."

SUCCESSFUL TIMING

Proper timing is part feel and part logic. I was walking through a West Coast manufacturing plant with the president when he surprised me by saying, "The most important ability of a leader is timing."

Being in the right place at the right time often determines success. This isn't just luck (particularly for Calvinists).

Our emotions have a lot to do with our timing. If we are too anxious, we may fire someone too early. If we are afraid, we wait too long. My experience is that many more miss proper timing by being late than by being early. Fear of making a mistake is the culprit.

Genesco was thinking to start a public-relations program in New York. Maxey Jarman and I were having dinner with the public-relations executives, listening to their proposition. Afterward, walking down Fifth Avenue, he asked me what I thought. I told him I felt I needed more information before making a decision. He said, "Specifically what information do you need? I think you're just procrastinating." I said, "You're right. I'm scared of spending that much money."

I never forgot the question Maxey asked me. I've reworked it into three words: "Why not now?"

LISTENING TO THE SPIRIT

I was speaking one night at the Shrine Auditorium in Los Angeles to six thousand sales executives. I knew there was an hour-long cocktail party beforehand, so I figured I would need a quick way to connect with the audience. I knew some wonderful stories, slightly off-color, that would grab the group's attention and generate a big laugh. However, I didn't feel comfortable using them.

As I paced my hotel room, I bowed my head and said, "Lord, I won't do it, and if during my presentation the time seems right to give a witness I'll do it."

About halfway into my talk I sensed a little hiatus, a transition, a sense of "now." I said only a few words about my faith, but a holy hush came over the crowd. I knew something had happened.

They stood and applauded and recalled me to the platform, but I didn't feel worthy to go. I knew I hadn't done it alone.

FOR THE "OLD MAN" OR THE "NEW MAN"

Sometimes Christians ask me if I think psychology can be used with integrity in Christian situations. My answer is yes, provided you start with a firm understanding of what the new birth is and what it means to be a new creature in Christ.

There should be a difference in the way a Christian and a non-Christian approach psychology. The overriding question for the Christian is whether psychology is being used to develop what the apostle Paul called the "new man" or whether it is being used to revitalize the "old man" and make him more comfortable.

People like to have the old man made comfortable. They receive comfort from hearing of a God of love, an empathetic, caring counselor kind of God, a Santa Claus God, a God to whom you can quote, "Ask whatever you want," and get it. That is not prayer based on redemption but on greed.

When we make the old man comfortable, we deceive our listeners and sacrifice their welfare to our own desire for comfort.

JOY IN SACRIFICE

Christians should know the joy of giving as well as the need for giving. We give to satisfy our need to give, to respond to God for what he has given us. Giving cleanses our conscience.

I learned this lesson from my father, who was financially abused by the churches he served. He never made more than $3,000 a year, and yet he taught me to tithe. Not only did my dad tithe on his gross income, he gave a gift above the tithe. I've never forgotten his example. When I was making six dollars a week I tithed sixty cents. That made it easier to give when my income was in six figures.

There is a level beyond obedience in giving. It's joy. Once we feel the joy of giving, we have received the blessing of giving. I can't explain it, but there is a connection between joy and sacrifice.

CREATING THIRST

Dr. Howard Rome, the psychiatrist, once told me, "You don't understand motivation until you understand thirst. Motivation is satisfying a thirst."

With this insight I began to observe that many pastors present water to nonthirsty members. The person who doesn't want to understand Scripture doesn't listen even to the best teaching. Horses that are not thirsty can't be made to drink. Pastors who are thirsty to teach the Bible must find listeners who are thirsty to hear it. We must first recognize the lack of thirst and the need to create it before we give someone the satisfaction, which will then be gladly received.

EVERYONE IS MOTIVATED

We use the word "motivation" as if it were only forward motion at various speeds. This is a wrong understanding of motivation.

Those who are doing nothing are motivated to do nothing. Those who are active are motivated to be active. To motivate people who are motivated to do nothing, we have to overcome the first motivation in order to get them in a forward movement. I was told by a corporate president who manufactured railroad engines that the biggest problem was harnessing enough power to start the train rolling. Aircraft designers have to build enough power into plane engines to break the pull of gravity before they can power the flight itself.

As leaders we need to recognize that inertia is a motivation, not simply the lack of it.

TONGUE MANAGEMENT

In Scripture the tongue is referred to as fire, one of the greatest discoveries of mankind. By it we do many things. Yet unmanaged it becomes one of the most destructive. The management of the tongue starts with the management of the heart, for out of the heart the tongue speaks.

For the tongue to have freedom, the soul must have purity. It must be purged of pride, greed, hostility, or the poison of the heart will come out of the mouth.

HARVESTING YOUR MENTAL ACTIVITY

We would hardly think of growing wheat without garnering it or tending fruit trees without picking the fruit, yet so much of the harvest of our mental activity is lost because we lack a system for retaining it or warehousing it.

For many years, I have kept a dictation machine nearby, supplemented by pen and paper, to record what I see, hear, observe, think, and read. I record stories, phrases, metaphors, thoughts that need additional exploration, beautiful definitions, and well-turned phrases. I have been doing this for more than sixty years. I not only collect what I believe but what opposes my belief, for I think opposition is helpful to our thought processes. It is said that writers see more. I think *perceive* would be a better word, for perception comes in so many different ways.

Not only does recording assure retention, but it correctly remembers. Practice gives us the ability to see and hear much more accurately.

Former Senate chaplain Dick Halverson at the first of every year made fifty files for the Sundays he would preach. This meant he had someplace to file everything he ran across. He sorted once, not fifty times.

TREATING THE WEALTHY WITH LOVE

The Book of James tells us not to treat the rich any differently than the poor, yet I'll guarantee you a known millionaire can't go to a church where he isn't courted. Such attitudes toward money can seriously erode a leader's integrity.

Better to say to the rich person, "I have a scriptural injunction not to be influenced by your wealth. I know that in all areas of life wealth is power. It receives respect. It is catered to, even in the church. But I know you want me to be a person of integrity, and if I am, then I've got to treat you as just another member. I'm interested in your soul much more than I am in your wealth. If you see me treating you differently than others, would you be kind enough to remind me of my responsibility to you?"

I must also say to this person, "Now, my treating you the same as every other member does not decrease your responsibility to give according to your wealth. If I preach tithing, I have to preach tithing to you."

Before I could say such a thing, however, I would need to earn my right to talk to him. I would want him to know I'm interested in him as a person. Then I could say to him with integrity, "If you ever went broke, you would be just as important in the church as you are today. Your wealth does not display or affect God's love for you."

The wealthy person needs this kind of honesty and love.

THE VALUE OF "I DON'T KNOW"

Recently a wealthy young man came to me with some problems in an area beyond my expertise. After listening a bit, I said, "I have no experience with what you're talking about."

"You have an opinion, don't you?" he responded.

I said, "I would hope I'm considerate enough not to give you an opinion in an area in which I have no knowledge. I'd like my opinion to be worth something, and I have no opinion that is worth anything regarding your situation."

He was disappointed, but I felt good about my response. I was afraid that if I gave him my opinion, because of his respect for me he would have taken it as advice.

There are times I say to myself, in effect, *I don't belong in this situation.* I can't let someone's disappointment or my ego throw me off course. Integrity demands I stay with the things I can do and do well.

How many times have you asked directions from someone who didn't know but wouldn't admit he didn't know? His ego and ignorance sent you on a wild goose chase.

Parting Comments

In parting, may I remind you: Our lives are more than our ministry. Our ministry is an outward evidence of Christ's redemption. Our call is to him, not just to work for him.

We read, study, and pray to maintain spiritual vitality, not only to serve but to be—with integrity.

I hope that what I have observed in my long life and recorded for your use will primarily build you internally, so that you can effectively use your skills increasingly for the Lord's glory, that your calling may be sure and not deteriorate into a mere religious profession.

As the sister of a young gang member said to him when he professed Christ, "Be real, man, be real."

Appendix

Fred Smith's Quotes on Life and Leadership

Good leadership is not domination. It serves through mutual benefit.

In every significant event there has been a bold leader, a shared vision, and, most often, an adversary.

Historian Will Durant said in *The Mansions of Philosophy*, "The masses do not accomplish much. They follow the lead of exceptional men."

A healthy society is one in which opportunities are given for leaders to emerge from all ranks of the society.

True leaders have a uniqueness that must be recognized and utilized.

No sluggard can succeed in leadership. There are passive persons who are content to go through life getting lifts from people, who wait until action is forced upon them. They are not leaders.

Leaders stay in front by raising the standards by which they judge themselves and by which they are willing to be judged.

A true leader loves excellence.

The leader carries with him a sense of idealism and imparts to others a vision of what might be.

A leader will take counsel from his people before he takes action but will act on what he sees as right. He has trained himself out of the fear of making mistakes.

Leadership requires courage. Once a leader decides his part in life and his endowments and responsibilities, he then acts with courage to tackle the problems.

There is responsibility in privilege. Leaders need to hold themselves to a stricter discipline than is expected of others. Those who are first in place must be first in merit.

No one is qualified to lead until he has learned the art of obeying.

Leaders are not capricious. They balance emotional drive and sound thinking. Possibilities stimulate their energy.

Ultimately, it is the force of character that inspires others to follow with confidence. A rogue may get you to eat ice cream but not to take distasteful medicine.

Authority may be delegated but not responsibility. Work done by others is the responsibility of the leader.

A leader needs to know to whom he may delegate and to whom he must only assign.

Leadership consists in getting people to work with, not for, you, particularly when they are under no obligation to do so.

Whoever is under a leader's direction should be under his protection.

Just trust me" isn't enough for long-term, effective action. Lord Montgomery, as commander of the Eighth Army, made it a rule that the plan of a campaign should be made known to every soldier.

Every element of the task should be simplified as much as possible. Remember, I repeat, Einstein said, "Whatever God does, he does in its simplest form." Leaders need the humility of simplicity, a simplicity developed beyond complexity, not before it.

A leader should see things whole as well as in parts. Often a leader must sacrifice his love of a specialty to the overall accomplishment of the vision.

Every decision should be evaluated on risk to reward. Longtime winners play with the odds, not against them.

An accomplishing leader originates and innovates. The "maintenance" leader protects status quo.

An effective leader combines logic, experience, intuition, and advice.

Self-advancement is not a proper goal for the spiritual leader.

Never expect others to work as hard as the leader unless they are profiting in satisfaction the same way he is.

An informed leader stays on the grapevine and off the rumor mill.

Wisdom has an amazing ability to escape the human mind.

Intelligent leaders profit from their mistakes by not repeating them.

A leader should look for what is wrong, not to criticize it but to correct it.

Worthwhile people are seeking to share a great purpose in life.

Never complain about a lack of time until you are equaling or exceeding the greatest people of history. They all had the same amount of time.

There are many psychological barriers in life. A leader learns to break these for individuals just as Roger Bannister broke the four-minute mile barrier. Others then are able to do what they never were able to do before.

At any given time, there are those institutions that are succeeding and those that are failing in the same industry or ministry. The difference is leadership.

When you plateau and start going around the same circle year after year, you are old, no matter what your age.

Until you accept the bad as a fact, you cannot enjoy the good as a possibility.

*T*hose who want no fences are generally predators, not good neighbors.

*T*hose who yearn for wisdom generally find it. Those who wish for it, miss it.

*T*he Prodigal Son found that purchased friendship was fleeting.

*T*ime preserves heroes and dissolves celebrities.

*C*hoice is the essence of character, because it is the evidence.

*D*r. S. I. Hayakawa, the general semanticist, told me, "Trust a man's actions more than his words."

*G*ratitude is one of the most fragile emotions. The Scripture praises the sacrifice of thanksgiving. Until we are grateful for what we have, how can we deserve to have more?

*T*he greatest aid in life is the presence of the Spirit. When you have a guide, you don't need a map.

*P*ray that God does not reveal your stupidity to you until you understand his grace.

*H*umor can often open the most closed mind.

*W*e express our values by our choices.

*G*enerally, unction accomplishes much more than eloquence.

*G*oebbels, Hitler's propaganda minister, understood the mass mind. He said, "Say it simply and repeat it often."

*F*ailures must be recognized as soon as possible. It is better to bury a corpse than to perfume it.

*T*he proper use of words is to effect worthwhile accomplishment.

*N*ever institute a policy that you cannot enforce. It weakens leadership.

*J*oy is a verification of a right relationship with God.

*N*ever capriciously criticize those in power.

*T*he best defense of the faith is a personification not an argument.

*N*ever be theologically naïve enough to believe that right always wins.

*S*ometimes the deepest, most serious truth comes dressed in humor.

*P*oor timing is the worst misuse of humor.

*I*n our society, money is the only thing that is its own reason for being. That is not new. Ecclesiastes says, "Money cures all things." It is a statement of what is, not what should be.

*I*t is good fortune when the passionate are also right.

*H*umor is the great defrocker of pomposity. It is still funny to see a snowball hit a top hat.

*H*umor can be a fine servant but an awesome tyrant. Never sacrifice a relationship for a laugh. A good test is,

"While the audience is laughing, are the angels weeping?"

Blue humor lets others see into your basement window.

The surest way to burn out is to take on jobs that do not fit your gifts, interest, or motivation.

Envy is the magnifying glass through which we look at the faults of others.

Family members and close friends are able to evaluate character much more than talent.

The ritual that becomes routine soon becomes a rut.

Patience is a valuable element, and I find that I have so much more with myself than I do for others.

I am not theologically educated, but I have found it a safe practice to teach only those principles that I can find personified in Scripture.

I have known some wonderful termites eating away at the devil's building.

The question is not "Is the speech a good one?" but "Is it an effective one?" Speak to change attitudes and behavior.

It is prostitution to use your supposed connection with God as a persuasion tool. The prophets were willing to risk their lives on their word from God. Do we treat it lightly?

people are saying to maintain conversation.

Using our discernment to lead requires much more. The following are ways to interpret what people are actually saying:

1. *Manifest listening.* First we listen for the meaning of words, both dictionary and colloquial. For example, young people today say "bad" when they mean "exceptionally good" (e.g., "He's a bad cat").

I am always surprised when people do not ask the meaning of words they don't know. I have never known a really intelligent person who will let you use a word he or she doesn't know without stopping to ask its meaning.

Next we listen to the selection of words, which can be intellectual or emotional. Then comes the pace, the speed with which a person speaks. Then the rhythm, which is the peaks and valleys.

Then the tone of the words. Tone is greatly indicative of the emotions.

It is helpful also to notice the manipulation of words (e.g., as it is done by the Washington spin doctors and the media).

Psychiatrists listen for glitches in the use of words. One psychiatrist told me that when we have a glitch it is generally because two ideas collide, and he is interested in which idea was suppressed and which was expressed.

I have found it is important to listen to the tone of slang, vulgarity, or profanity. The tone tells me whether it's intentional or a habit, whether it's a tool or just an expression.

The use of words and accents often gives us a glimpse into someone's past. The drummer Buddy Rich told me that he could hear a player's history when he heard how he